Learning Centers

Jodi L. McClay, M.A.

Teacher Created Materials, Inc.

Cover Design by Darlene Spivak

Copyright © 1996 Teacher Created Materials, Inc. All rights reserved.

No part of this publication may be reproduced in whole or in part, or stored in any retrieval system, or transmitted in any form or by any means, electronic, mechanical, photocopying, recording, or otherwise, without written permission from the publisher, Teacher Created Materials, Inc., 6421 Industry Way, Westminster, CA 92683.

Made in U.S.A.

ISBN 1-55734-891-X

Order Number TCM 891

Table of Contents

Introduction i

Overview of Learning Centers 1

Getting Started 15

Planning Activities 31

Classroom Management 43

Student Accountability 61

Authentic Assessment 65

References 75

Introduction

All children are special. Each has unique talents, interests, and learning style preferences; no two are alike. Yet, historically, teachers have routinely provided *classroom* instruction and assessment in an effort to meet the needs of the group rather than individual students. They have incorrectly assumed that all students in the classroom will benefit from the same course of study. Or, perhaps, they have recognized that not every child is ready for the same learning experience, but they have not received the direction and encouragement necessary to embark on a journey to individualize curriculum.

How is it possible to individualize the curriculum? With increasingly large class sizes and few resources for assistance, can teachers truly meet the needs of each and every student? At first glance it may seem futile to attempt to teach to anything other than "the middle," but a deeper introspection shows the fallacy of this approach. Advanced students quickly become bored, while children who need more time or practice are frustrated and often humiliated in front of their peers. There is, in fact, no "middle;" students must be respected as unique individuals with specific strengths and needs. As teachers, we must respect individual learning styles and establish positive learning objectives that meet each child's needs.

The use of learning centers is becoming a popular way to meet the academic, social, emotional, and physical needs of elementary students. Teachers are not longer expecting students to sit passively, listen to lectures, and regurgitate information on paper-and-pencil exams. Instead, they are recognizing that students learn best when they are actively involved in the learning process. Learning centers enable classrooms to decentralize and become student-centered rather than teacher-directed.

What are learning centers? How are they planned, implemented, and managed? How are students held accountable? Is authentic assessment possible? This book will answer these questions plus many more. It will provide an in-depth look at the rationale for learning centers and the research based on such programs. In addition, it will describe the steps for reorganizing the classroom to accommodate a learning center approach, determining appropriate activities, and monitoring student choices and progress. Enjoy!

Overview of Learning Centers

History
Traditionally, classroom instruction has centered around rows of neatly lined desks where students sit passively listening to teacher-directed lessons. The scope and sequence of these lessons have addressed the needs of the class majority, the average. Students in the minority, those working above or below expectations, often responded with boredom, withdrawal, or frustration. Regardless of interest or ability, students were expected to pay close attention to the teacher, take copious notes, and regurgitate information under test conditions. Unfortunately, this approach to teaching and learning has dominated American classrooms for decades, and it has resulted in an educational atmosphere of rigidity that fails to stimulate creativity, lacks concern for individual talents and differences, and rewards mediocrity.

An alternative to this traditional approach is an active teaching-learning environment that utilizes learning centers. Learning centers provide children with endless opportunities to explore concepts in a variety of ways. They facilitate an educational approach that

> **Learning centers provide children with endless opportunities to explore concepts in a variety of ways.**

respects individual learning styles and abilities, enhances cooperative learning and teamwork skills, and shifts focus from teaching to learning. Learning centers spark interests and raise self-esteem by letting children take charge of their own learning; they provide opportunities for each and every student to excel.

What Is a Learning Center?

For purposes of classroom instruction, "learning center" is often used synonymously with other phrases such as learning station, work booth, and free-choice activity. Another common association, however, is that of the resource center in the library; often this is referred to as The Learning Center, a place where students go for tutorial assistance. In fact, while conducting research for this book, nearly all of the articles and information on learning centers referred to those found in the library. Unfortunately, while there are many resource books for learning center tasks, the ideas behind using learning centers in the classroom have received little attention.

Definition

A learning center is a special area in the classroom where students can work independently or in small groups to build a concept, explore a topic, or refine a skill. Consider the old Chinese proverb:

> I hear, and I forget,
>
> I see, and I remember,
>
> I do, and I understand.

Learning centers support this proverb, as well as John Dewey's philosophy that "learning is doing" (Pattillo & Vaughan, 1992). They require little or no teacher direction. The teacher becomes a facilitator and observer, while students learn by activity rather than passivity.

A learning center can be as simple as a magnet lying on a table or as complex as an entire discovery lesson with directions and questions for analysis. Centers can have specific learning objectives for each student or simply provide students with opportunities for exploration and inquiry. Learning centers allow students to work creatively, independently, and in small groups; they are based on the premise that students need and deserve the freedom to explore and inquire in a manner that is comfortable for them.

In order for students to construct knowledge that is meaningful to them, most successful centers focus on reinforcement or enrichment. That is, they do not attempt to introduce new concepts or informa-

> **A learning center can be as simple as a magnet lying on a table or as complex as an entire discovery lesson with directions and questions for analysis.**

tion. Rather, they serve to review and provide additional opportunities for enrichment by supporting what is being taught in the classroom (Pfau & Zeddun, 1995; Wallace, 1993). They also have a variety of activities that accommodate different learning styles and interests (Johnston, James, Barnes, & Colton, 1978). Sample learning center activities can be found on pages 4 through 6. These particular tasks are designed for primary students yet are effective for older students reviewing the concept, as well.

Sample Activity

Level: Second Grade

Literature: *The Doorbell Rang*

Author & Illustrator: Pat Hutchins

Publisher: Mulberry Books, New York, 1986

Purpose: to introduce students to the concept of division

Materials

- at least one copy of the literature selection
- one copy of each of the two activity sheets (pages 5 and 6)
- scissors
- glue
- crayons (if students wish to color the cookies)

Preparation

- Reproduce copies of the activity sheets for each student.
- Write the instructions for the activity on a chart for students.
- Make samples if you think it is necessary.

Instructions

- Introduce the concept of division by reading the literature selection to students.
- Explain to them that they will have to divide up the cookies evenly among people on the activity sheet at the learning center.

Reprinted from TCM 790 Teaching Basic Skills Through Literature: Math, *Teacher Created Materials, 1995*

Math Center Activity Sheet #1

You have made six cookies. Two of your friends come over to eat the cookies with you. Divide the cookies evenly among you and your friends by cutting and gluing them in each of the boxes.

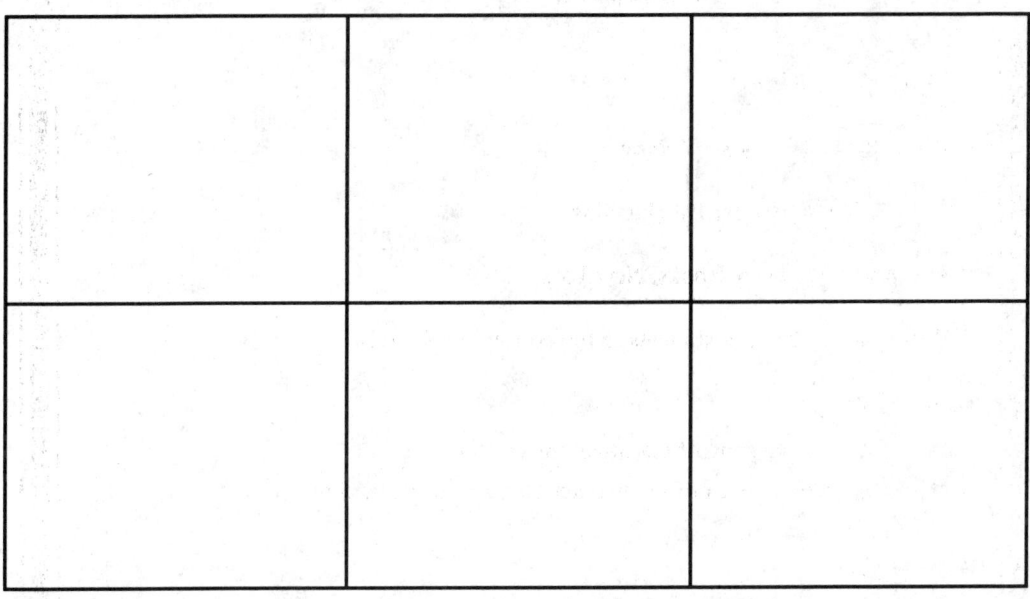

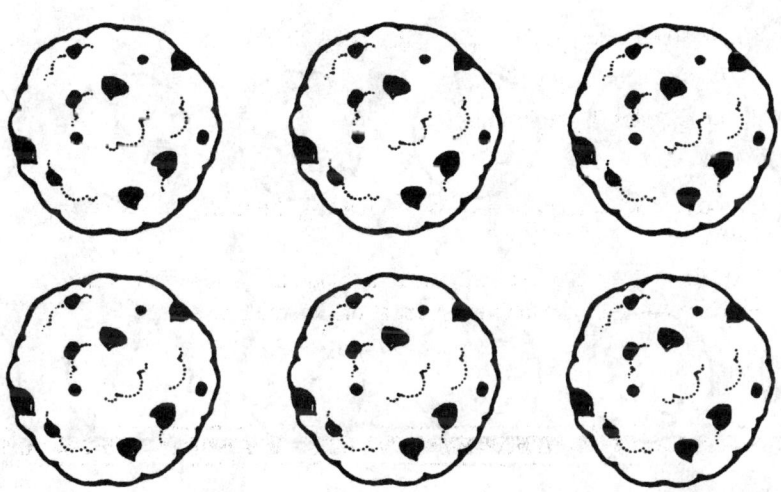

Reprinted from TCM 790 Teaching Basic Skills Through Literature: Math, *Teacher Created Materials, 1995*

Math Center Activity Sheet #2

You have made twelve cookies. Five of your friends come over to eat the cookies with you. Divide the cookies up evenly among you and your friends by cutting and gluing them in each of the boxes.

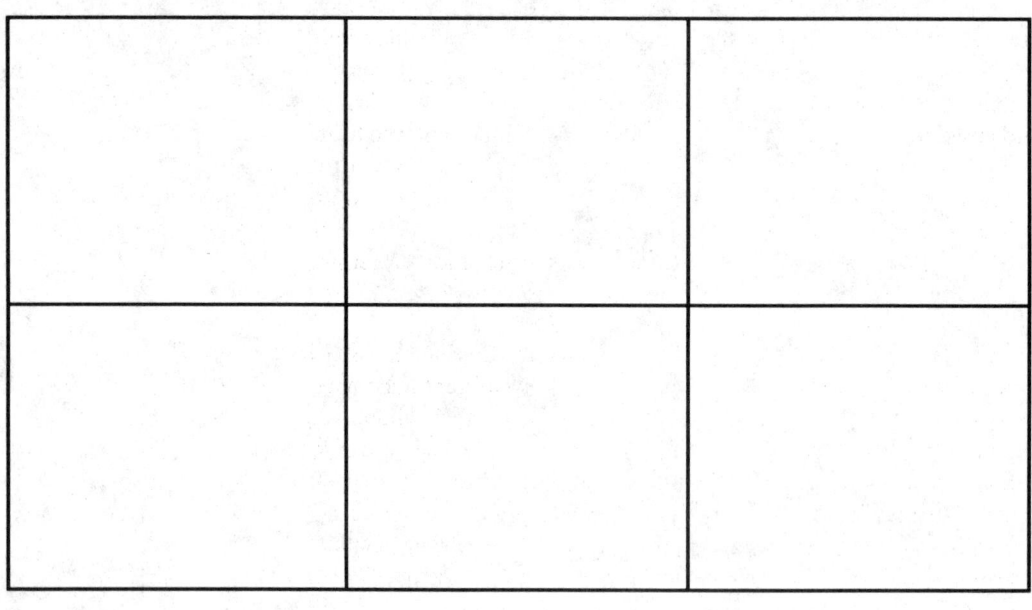

- -

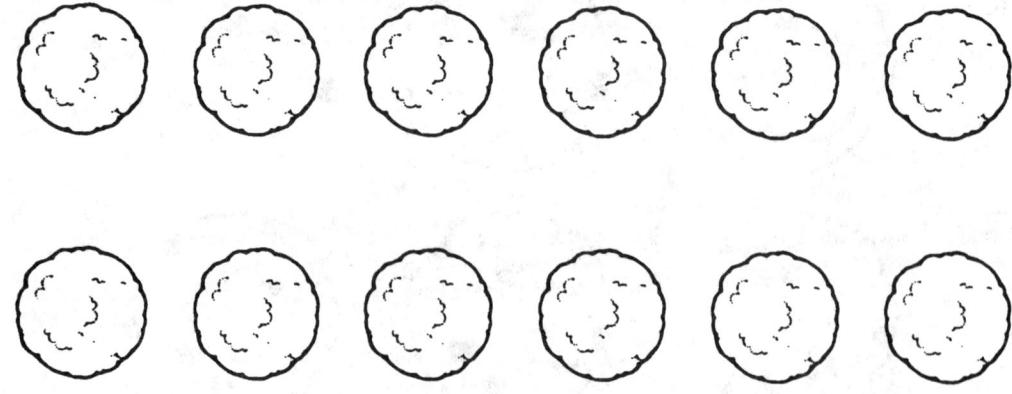

Reprinted from TCM 790 Teaching Basic Skills Through Literature: Math, *Teacher Created Materials, 1995*

When Should Learning Centers Be Used?

It is important to remember that learning centers are not to be utilized by just students who have finished their assigned work. Many teachers provide this "free-choice" time for students who have completed their assignments. Do not be fooled! A valuable learning center must be accessible to all students. This "free-choice" approach deprives many students the opportunities to investigate, review, and explore interests. A child who may complete written tasks more slowly than others deserves and needs the chance to work in centers. In fact, this particular child may benefit immensely from working in another domain. Rather than utilizing learning centers just with students who have finished work considered more important, use learning centers as a vehicle to provide important work for every student. The following chapter presents many learning center models to use in the classroom. Adopt an approach that is comfortable for you while permitting all students to benefit from participation in learning centers.

A valuable learning center must be accessible to all students.

What Does a Learning Center Classroom Look Like?

A learning center classroom looks significantly different in comparison to a traditional setting. Rows of desks and passive children are replaced by a busy classroom that thrives on active learning. Students work independently and collaboratively on a variety of activities and at many locations. The environment is often noisier than a traditional setting, as students become responsible for their learning and take an active part in the planning and evaluation processes. Learning center teachers "must function more like orchestra conductors than like lecturers: getting things started and keeping them moving along, providing information and pointing to resources, coordinating a diverse but harmonious buzz of activity" (Goodlad & Oakes, 1988, p. 19). An observer of a primary classroom and an upper grade classroom might see the following centers in operation on a given day:

Grade 1	Grade 5
Math Center	Computation Center
Construction Center	Problem Solving Center
Music Center	Discovery Science Center
Social Studies Center	Computer Center
Science Center	Dramatic Play Center
Writing Center	Brainstorming Center
Spelling Center	Rough Draft Center
Art Center	Peer Editing Center
Listening Center	Publishing/Computer Center
Reading Center	Puzzle Center

Do not be alarmed! To some people, the thought of having so many activities going on at one time is overwhelming. However, what you will find as you continue reading is that learning centers provide more student ownership, peer tutoring, and time for the teacher to deliver quality instruction to one or few students at a time. The chapter entitled Classroom Management will include valuable ideas for creating such an environment. The sample diagrams in the following chapter, Getting Started, will provide a visual image of a classroom rich with learning centers.

Rationale for Learning Centers

The advantages of learning centers are many! Teachers who have made the transition from traditional teacher-directed activities to student-initiated learning centers are ecstatic over the results. The following benefits are convincing many teachers to join in:

◆ Student Autonomy
◆ Concrete Experiences
◆ Peer Tutoring
◆ Cooperative Learning
◆ Individualization
◆ Better Use of Resources
◆ Opportunities for Teacher

Student Autonomy

The use of learning centers in the classroom rests on the notion that students are capable of working independently, or cooperatively, without the teacher's direct involvement. Rather than assuming that the teacher is the primary resource for knowledge, learning centers give ownership and autonomy to the students. They encourage individuality, facilitate learning styles and preferences, and accommodate varied rates of learning. Learning centers provide opportunities where children can create knowledge and understanding themselves.

As autonomous learners, students begin to self-pace and self-evaluate. While these are not easy strategies to learn, they are vital for success. The ability to set one's pace is a skill most individuals do not master until adulthood; learning centers, however, encourage students to take responsibility for their accomplishments. Students enjoy the freedom to set time limits, plan projects, and revise time lines, if needed. Most upper grade teachers incorporate student-initiated projects into learning centers. Meeting regularly with the teacher, students must set and reach goals in a manner congruent with that of the teacher's expectations. Naturally, self-evaluation

> **Learning centers provide opportunities where children can create knowledge and understanding themselves.**

skills are also included. The most common are writing prompts such as:

> *"Do you believe that your writing journal shows progress? Why?"*
> *"What was your most valuable math exercise this semester? Why?"*
> *"Why have you chosen this piece of work for your portfolio?"*
> *"What have you learned at the Science Center lately? How did you arrive at this knowledge?"*

When students become the "directors," trusted with the important task of learning, they are guided into understanding self-pacing and self-evaluation. No longer is it the responsibility of the teacher to inform students of their progress. Students now understand the importance of self-evaluation as a necessity for future goals.

A big portion of being "autonomous" has to do with having choices. Learning centers provide choices! Whether it be which center to attend, whom to work with, how long to work at a center, or what to do while there, learning centers provide opportunities to choose, and choices are vital ingredients in learning and critical thinking.

As students become more autonomous, levels of self-esteem rise dramatically. Students learn that they can progress as quickly as they like, and they assume responsibility for learning. A perfect example is "John," a fourth grade student who entered the classroom extremely withdrawn and depressed. John's reading and writing skills were pre-first grade level, and he expressed in many ways his belief that he was incapable of functioning in the classroom. However, what John did not realize was that his new teacher's method of providing instruction was different from that of his old teacher. He was no longer required to listen to lengthy lectures and be laughed at when called upon to read. Instead, he was able to work individually with the teacher during reading and writing centers, tutor primary students in the afternoon, and work with peers to explore new information at learning centers of interest. The teacher individualized most of the center activities and grouped John with children of similar interests. When activities called for peer collaboration, ability levels were varied. This approach allowed John to learn at his pace and ability without being labeled. In so doing, his self-esteem immediately increased, and he began to explore new social situations, as well.

Concrete Experiences

Learning centers provide the opportunities to learn with real objects (Pattillo & Vaughan, 1992; Thomas, 1975). Rather than reading in a science textbook about the properties of matter, students are able to experiment and explore with real solids, liquids, and gases. They need to form their own understandings and arrive at solutions based on their experiences, not those of textbook authors. Learning centers provide these opportunities. They enable children to explore and create knowledge.

Peer Tutoring

In a learning center classroom, students learn from each other through peer tutoring. As they work together to explore and experiment, students assist one another in creating knowledge and understanding. This is a significant advantage to learning centers, because as most will agree, there is no better way to truly learn a topic than to teach it. In fact, research shows that only 10% of students are capable of learning by reading from a textbook; in contrast, 90% are able to learn if they are actively teaching others (Glasser, 1990).

In a learning center classroom, students learn from each other through peer tutoring.

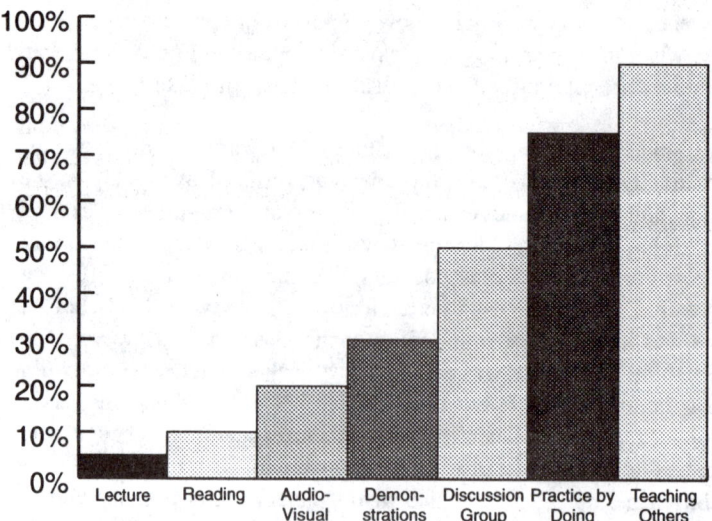

How Students Learn

Cooperative Learning

The use of learning centers enables students to work collaboratively, and it affords excellent opportunities to build cooperative learning skills. Students develop the social skills necessary to live and work with people of different abilities, interests, and backgrounds. They are given early experiences to work with colleagues, share ideas, give suggestions, and compromise in order to reach a desired goal. An excellent example of a cooperative group activity is on page 12.

Individualization

Variety in instruction is important. Research shows that individual learning styles vary, and students learn best if more than one method of instruction is utilized (Lazear, 1991). Learning centers enable the teacher to individualize the curriculum and meet each child's needs. For instance, a math center rich in manipulatives, objects, and games can accommodate students of all levels. An individualized approach, where students attending the math center have specific lessons designed for their needs, is an extremely popular and effective way to provide quality experiences for students of various levels.

At first glance, the thought of preparing specific lessons for each student might appear very time consuming. However, most teachers find it far less difficult than anticipated, because students begin to propose their own projects and work with peers to design surveys and problems. The teacher spends most of the time as a facilitator, conferencing with students on proposed or finished work; in fact, there is often time to present quality instruction to individual or small groups of children on a daily basis.

Better Use of Resources

With fewer students using materials at once, less becomes more. For instance, if only four students are in the science center, only four magnifying glasses are needed. Instead of purchasing a class set, the teacher is able to spend limited funds on additional items (Opitz, 1994).

Story Map

This is a story map. Can you guess the name of the fairy tale?

Try making a map of the book you have read.

Directions:

1. Think of some important events in your story.
2. Tell about each picture.
3. Color the pictures.
4. Cut them out.
5. Glue them on a large sheet of paper.
6. Draw arrows to make a path from one picture to the next.

Share your map with a friend. Ask if he or she can guess the name of your story.

To the teacher: This can also be used as a cooperative learning project with a group of children working together to create a large story map. If you supply markers and die, creative children may be encouraged to turn this project into a game.

Reprinted from TCM 147 Activities for Any Literature Unit, *Teacher Created Materials, 1995*

Opportunities for Teachers

Teachers using learning centers in the classroom have many more opportunities to truly meet the needs of each student than teachers in traditional settings. Rather than providing the same instruction for the entire class, learning centers allow teachers to present the curriculum to a wide range of abilities and learning styles.

Current research has identified seven different intelligences within each individual, linguistic, logical-mathematical, spatial, bodily-kinesthetic, musical, interpersonal, and intrapersonal. According to Gardner's multiple intelligence theory, each individual possesses all seven intelligences to varying degrees and therefore responds better when instruction is directed to one of the dominant areas (Gardner, 1985).

The use of learning centers encourages teachers to individualize instruction based on these multiple intelligences. A wonderful example is "Alexa," a second grade student with extreme talent and intelligence in the area of spatial intelligence. Alexa had trouble with writing and reading. Her spelling was extremely poor; her word attack skills were low, as well. Though Alexa lacked confidence in reading and writing, she absolutely loved to draw and share her creations with others. Her portraits were beautiful, utilizing dimension, color, and space. Alexa also exhibited high intelligence in the area of interpersonal intelligence. She expressed great love for her classmates, enjoyed learning and sharing information on diversities and differences, and was a leader in cooperative group activities. In the classroom, the teacher was able to match Alexa's dominant areas of intelligence with learning center activities. Alexa was encouraged to draw pictures to interpret information, highlight text in color, and take time to visualize and create. She was given opportunities to help others in team projects and peer tutoring.

The use of learning centers encourages teachers to individualize instruction based on these multiple intelligences.

Learning centers also provide a system in which the teacher can work with small groups of students while other children are actively learning. Traditionally, teachers rarely met with small groups of students as they were busy directing lessons to the entire class; when they did work with a few students at one time, other classmates were doing what most classify as "busy work," paper-and-pencil tasks designed to keep them busy. Learning centers, however, free the teacher to work with individuals or small groups of students while other students enjoy authentic learning experiences.

As students become autonomous individuals engaged in active learning experiences, another wonderful opportunity arises for the teacher—time to observe and assess students' learning. Most teachers who start learning centers are quickly amazed at the time they have to actually watch students process information. This valuable assessment is then used to plan and revise learning center activities for individual students. The last chapter, Authentic Assessment, provides excellent ideas for assessing students during learning centers.

What Does the Research Say?

Before starting learning centers, many teachers ask, "What does the research say?" This is an important concern because quality instructional time is such an important asset for teachers. In fact, research affirms the value of learning centers and emphasizes several instructional advantages:

> **Teachers across the country are using learning centers as an effective and enjoyable way to engage students of various abilities and interests in active learning.**

- ◆ Learning centers address learning styles better than paper-and-pencil tasks; they also motivate students more by providing varied stimulating activities (Wait & Stephens, 1989).
- ◆ Learning centers result in improved communication between home and school (Opitz, 1995).
- ◆ Learning centers play an important role in meeting the needs of each child, even those with special needs (Huyett, 1994).
- ◆ Learning centers are a vital part of a collaborative classroom. They offer students choice and contribute to a supportive, nurturing learning environment (Routman, 1991).

Concluding Remarks

Teachers across the country are using learning centers as an effective and enjoyable way to engage students of various abilities and interests in active learning. As small, inviting areas of the classroom designed for only one or a few students at a time, learning centers encourage student autonomy, increase self-esteem, provide concrete learning experiences, and develop cooperative learning skills. They allow the teacher to individualize the curriculum and assess student progress more authentically. Most importantly, learning centers teach students to think critically, make decisions, solve problems, and demonstrate personal characteristics of responsibility, self-management, and integrity. All of these attributes meet the standards of *What Work Requires of Schools: A SCANS Report for America 2000* (United States Department of Labor, 1994). Perhaps if we can align our classroom goals with those required to be productive citizens, our students can have a brighter future.

Getting Started

Review Your Beliefs
The first step in any change process is to examine your philosophy of how children learn. Making the transition to learning centers should not be based on an administrator's wish or the desire to be more like another teacher. It must be a choice based on personal beliefs about what type of environment best suits the needs of students. The amount of time and effort needed to establish successful learning centers will be worthwhile only if the philosophical reasons behind the change are complementary.

To see if learning centers are the best option for you, ask yourself the following questions:

- ◆ How do I think children learn best?
- ◆ What are the most important things children need to learn?
- ◆ What is my role as the teacher in the learning process?
- ◆ What can I do to ensure success for all students?

> **The first step in any change process is to examine your philosophy of how children learn.**

After you have reviewed your beliefs, it should be clear whether or not learning centers will best suit your needs and the needs of your students. If you believe the teacher's role is to be the sole planner, presenter, and evaluator of the curriculum and student progress, learning centers are probably not a good place to devote your time. If, on the other hand, you feel that children construct knowledge from interactions with others and explorations with materials and that students should be responsible, self-directed individuals, then you will find learning centers to be an excellent vehicle for such development (Pattillo & Vaughan, 1992).

How Will Learning Centers Be Used?

The first thing that needs to be decided is the extent to which learning centers will be utilized in the classroom. While many teachers use learning centers as the primary source of learning and for a great deal of time each day, it is necessary to find the right balance for you. One suggestion is to begin with a set of centers for a particular subject or theme and rotate students on a scheduled basis. Such an approach gives both the teacher and students an opportunity to experience centers before making a total commitment. A decision to try this could look like any of the following examples where students are divided into five heterogeneous groups and rotate to a new center each day:

Math Centers	Reading Centers	Theme Centers
9:45–10:30 Daily	8:15–9:45 Daily	"OUTER SPACE" 1:45–2:30 Daily
Measurement Center—with many activities	Listening Center—story response activity	Research Center—Locate and make fact cards about the planets
Geoboard Designs Center: Create 1" shapes	Computer Center *ReadingMaze*™	Writing Center—Make-Believe 2" Story: "If I Went to Outer Space ..."
Computer Center—*Math Blaster* or *Number Maze*®	Reading Game—Sight Word Bingo	Math Center—Work as a group to make a poster of the solar system (to scale).
Teacher Directed Lesson—Introduction to quarter-inch	Poem Sequencing—with sentence strips	Music Center—Write and perform "Spacey Songs" to the tune of nursery rhymes.
Individualized Math Books—Practice measuring to the half and quarter-inch.	Quiet Reading—Literature journal response	Listening Center—*The Magic School Bus Inside the Solar System* (Cole, 1990)

Easing into centers using one of the above models has been very effective for many teachers. Most report that by focusing on just one area and one period of time, they are better able to prepare quality center activities and train students to become autonomous, self-directed individuals. (Training students to become autonomous, self-directed individuals is an incredible task and will be discussed at length in the chapter entitled Classroom Management.)

How Many Centers Will Be Used?

Another important decision must be made in terms of the number of centers that will operate at any one time. The primary factor in this decision should be the number of students you want working at each location. While some centers may vary in the number of students who can be accommodated, a general way to prepare is to divide the total number of students in the class by the number of students desired at each center. For example, in a class of twenty-eight students, four learning centers are needed if the teacher desires no more than seven students working at each location. Similarly, if the teacher wants only four students working at each center, seven centers will be necessary.

Some teachers wish to have just a few students at each area; some choose to have a center for each student. Though personal experience finds that this approach eliminates student interaction and collaboration, some teachers report that students take great pride in the individualization of their work and still enjoy sharing and working with peers on projects of interest. Regardless, it is strongly recommended that teachers and students new to learning centers begin with just a few until everyone has gained experience and becomes comfortable with the structure, expectations, and opportunities that learning centers offer.

A Primary Grade Model

One design that has been highly successful with young learners is the use of four learning centers in the morning time block. Using this approach, students are grouped in four heterogeneous groups and rotate through the centers every thirty minutes.

At each center, there are a variety of activities that may be occurring on a given day. At the Writing Center, for instance:

- ◆ Two students may be brainstorming for a story about ants.
- ◆ Two students may be peer-editing their rough draft reports.

> Some teachers wish to have just a few students at each area; some choose to have a center for each student.

- One student may be working on his or her handwriting as he or she recopies the story.
- One student may be reading his or her story to a student partner or parent.
- One student may be illustrating his published book.
- One student may be typing her revised story on the computer.
- One student may be conferencing with the teacher.

Students receive individualized attention amidst peer interaction at each location. Although there are only four centers in operation, there are "mini," individualized center activities occurring at some or all locations. In addition, the teacher can have all students at a center do the same activity. For instance, the reading center group may all be asked to listen and respond to the same story, or the math center may all play the same game as a review to a concept just introduced to the entire class. A sample week's plan for a primary class is diagrammed below:

Students receive individualized attention amidst peer interaction at each location.

Day 1	Day 2	Day 3	Day 4	Day 5
Math activity related to theme	Individualized math books	Individualized math books	Math game	Assessment activity
Journal writing	Write a story with a friend.	Publish day #2's cooperative story.	Write a poster advertisement for a book.	Journal writing
Listening center and paired response to theme story	Individualized reading	Reading game	Tape record reading samples.	Story sequencing
Free choice activities	Free choice activities	Free choice activities	Free choice activities	Free choice activities

This model can also accommodate the desire to have only one student working at each learning center. To do this, simply make one group the learning center group and allow them the opportunity to visit centers while the other three groups work on similar tasks, i.e., teacher-directed reading group, seatwork group, boardwork group, and learning center group (Poppe & Van Matre, 1985). Using this model, groups can rotate at specific times, allowing each group to finish all four each day or having each group complete only one per day, taking four days to finish the rotation. Primary teachers have found that this approach works well for one subject area and forty-five minute period daily; whereas, upper grade teachers seem to prefer spending more time and allowing students to complete all four each day.

Another option for easing into learning centers is the "one-day-a-week" model, where students enjoy learning center opportunities just one day each week (Thomas, 1975). "Fantastic Friday" or "Marvelous Monday" could have the following learning center options:

Reading Center Choices—Do 2

1. Read two stories to a friend.

2. Listen to the story tape and complete the sequencing activity. (Required)

3. Read to yourself and respond in your literature journal.

4. Design an "end-of-the-story" test for a book you have read.

Science Center Choices—Do 1

1. Explore with the magnet set and respond in your science journal.

2. Continue on a project.

3. Design a new experiment following the scientific method guidelines. (Present steps 1–3 to the teacher.)

Math Center Choices—Do 2

1. Complete one page in your math book. (Required)

2. Design a survey and present your proposal to the teacher.

> **This model can also accommodate the desire to have only one student working at each learning center.**

3. Play Multiplication Bingo.

Social Studies Center Choices—Do 2

1. Review today's school newspaper and complete a critique. (Required)

2. Work on your "local history" project.

3. Play *Oregon Trail* (MECC) on the computer.

Writing Center Choices—Do 2

1. Work in your writing journal. (Required)

2. Work with a partner or two to write a science fiction thriller.

3. Write an additional stanza for our "Poem of the Week."

Art Center Choices—Do 1

1. Create something!

2. Work with a partner and create an educational poster.

3. Use pastels to make a picture titled "The Sun Rises."

Though six are shown, let personal preference dictate how many centers to use and for how long. While this example would consume the entire day, some teachers recommend beginning with a modified model, using only a few centers for a half day.

A daily plan and individual work folders are excellent ways to monitor student choices and assess progress with all of the learning center models illustrated. These and other management strategies, such as a check-off list at each location to ensure full participation by all class members and signs to show how many students may work at each location, are vital components and will be highlighted in the Classroom Management and Student Accountability chapters.

Grouping Students

Many teachers who use learning centers avoid the pitfalls of grouping students by letting students choose their own partners. While this respects student choice, it can also limit social interactions and student progress, as well as make management extremely difficult. For that reason, most teachers assign students to particular groups,

> **Many teachers who use learning centers avoid the pitfalls of grouping students by letting students choose their own partners.**

although the extent of the groups varies. For instance, it is possible to allow students to work with whomever they choose yet meet with the teacher in assigned groups. Or, students can rotate through all of the centers in the same groupings. A drawback to this approach is that many teachers report behavior problems when students are consistently working with the same peers. Perhaps the best suggestion is to complete center rotations on a daily basis and to change group members each day. Before beginning centers, simply draw names out of a hat, call names, or accept volunteers to form each center. Then, rotate at the scheduled times, having students remain in the original groups. Students enjoy working with different students each day while teachers enjoy the opportunities to group students according to their wishes. Students can be grouped by interest, ability, need, or learning style, whatever the teacher wants for the day. The following day, groups will be entirely different, providing students the opportunity to work with as many peers as possible.

Another option is to group students on a weekly basis and have them complete one center rotation together each day. The following page can be of assistance when forming groups. It helps to balance each group according to achievement, special needs, and language. Depending on the teacher's needs, these variables can change. For example, some centers may be based on student needs, while others attempt to capitalize on all talents, taking into consideration gender, interest, ability, and attitude.

Selecting Cooperative Groups

Legend

    HA: High Achiever

    SN: Special Needs Student

    ESL: English as a Second Language Student

    CA: Competent Achiever

Group One (example)	Group Two	Group Three
(HA)	( )	( )
(CA)	( )	( )
(CA)	( )	( )
(SN)	( )	( )
(ESL)	( )	( )
Notes: _____ _____ _____	Notes: _____ _____ _____	Notes: _____ _____ _____

Group Four	Group Five	Group Six
( )	( )	( )
( )	( )	( )
( )	( )	( )
( )	( )	( )
( )	( )	( )
Notes: _____ _____ _____	Notes: _____ _____ _____	Notes: _____ _____ _____

Reprinted from TCM 651 Cooperative Learning Activities for Language Arts, *Teacher Created Materials, 1995*

Arranging the Classroom

There are many things to consider when arranging a learning center classroom. The first is that the room must be physically decentralized (Thomas, 1975). That is, control must be shifted from the teacher to the students. Desks cannot be lined in rows facing the chalkboard. Learning centers require active participation by all students. Therefore, students must have access to manipulatives, information, supplies, and peers. The room must accommodate these necessities and be an inviting, enjoyable environment conducive to learning.

Before moving furniture, make a sketch of the classroom and include all permanent fixtures, such as the sink, cupboards, and electrical outlets (Petreshene, 1978). Make several copies of the sketch and begin drawing ideas. Work with the outline, considering all of the following:

- ◆ Traffic flow—It saves time during rotation and helps maintain order if centers flow from one to the other. For example, if you want the Writing Center to follow the Listening Center so that students can respond to a story they heard, there needs to be a short distance between the two. Also, the direction should continue onto the next center, clockwise or counter-clockwise, so that students are not running into others as they rotate.

- ◆ Noisy and quiet areas—It is important that noisy centers not be placed near quiet centers, as students will experience disruptions. For example, do not place the Reading Center next to the Building Block Center, as once blocks are stacked, they usually fall. Similarly, a Game Center will interrupt students working on developing story ideas at a Brainstorming Center if placed too close in proximity. Try to arrange noisy centers together and quiet centers together.

- ◆ Whole group area—Even though students will be working individually or in small groups, a whole group meeting area is crucial for the entire class to meet. Shared reading, class meetings, and whole class instruction require an area. Select a cozy corner or carpeted area that is big enough for everyone to be comfortable but not so big that students lose the feeling of cohesiveness and become lost in a crowd.

- ◆ Storage space—Consider two things: first, that students need space for personal belongings such as jackets, notebooks, and backpacks. A learning center classroom does

> **It saves time during rotation and helps maintain order if centers flow from one to the other.**

not need a desk for each student and most likely will not have room for one once centers are set up for active learning. Therefore, teachers must be creative when it comes to personal storage space. Cupboards, laundry baskets, and even large coffee cans have been attached and stacked to create individual spaces. Second, there needs to be storage for many manipulatives and supplies. An art center must be filled with supplies to stimulate creativity; a math center must have the objects necessary to learn abstract concepts in a concrete manner. Consider where you will store materials and try to locate each center close to its manipulatives and supplies.

◆ Display areas —It is also helpful to have learning centers located near their display boards. For instance, if you have a large area used to display student writing samples, it is a good idea to place the Writing Center near it, as students will enjoy reading and sharing their stories with others. This will also assist other students in incorporating the modeled strategies into their work.

◆ Permanent fixtures—Though this may sound unimportant, do not be fooled! Teachers have been known to set up their entire classrooms before realizing that the only electrical outlet is thirty feet from the Computer Center, or the Art Center is on the opposite side of the room from the sink. Consider what is permanent and work around the limitations.

Two sample diagrams of learning center classrooms are on the following pages. Note the low-cost furniture and creative use of storage and dividers.

It is also helpful to have learning centers located near their display boards.

Learning Center Classroom Diagram
Grades 1–3

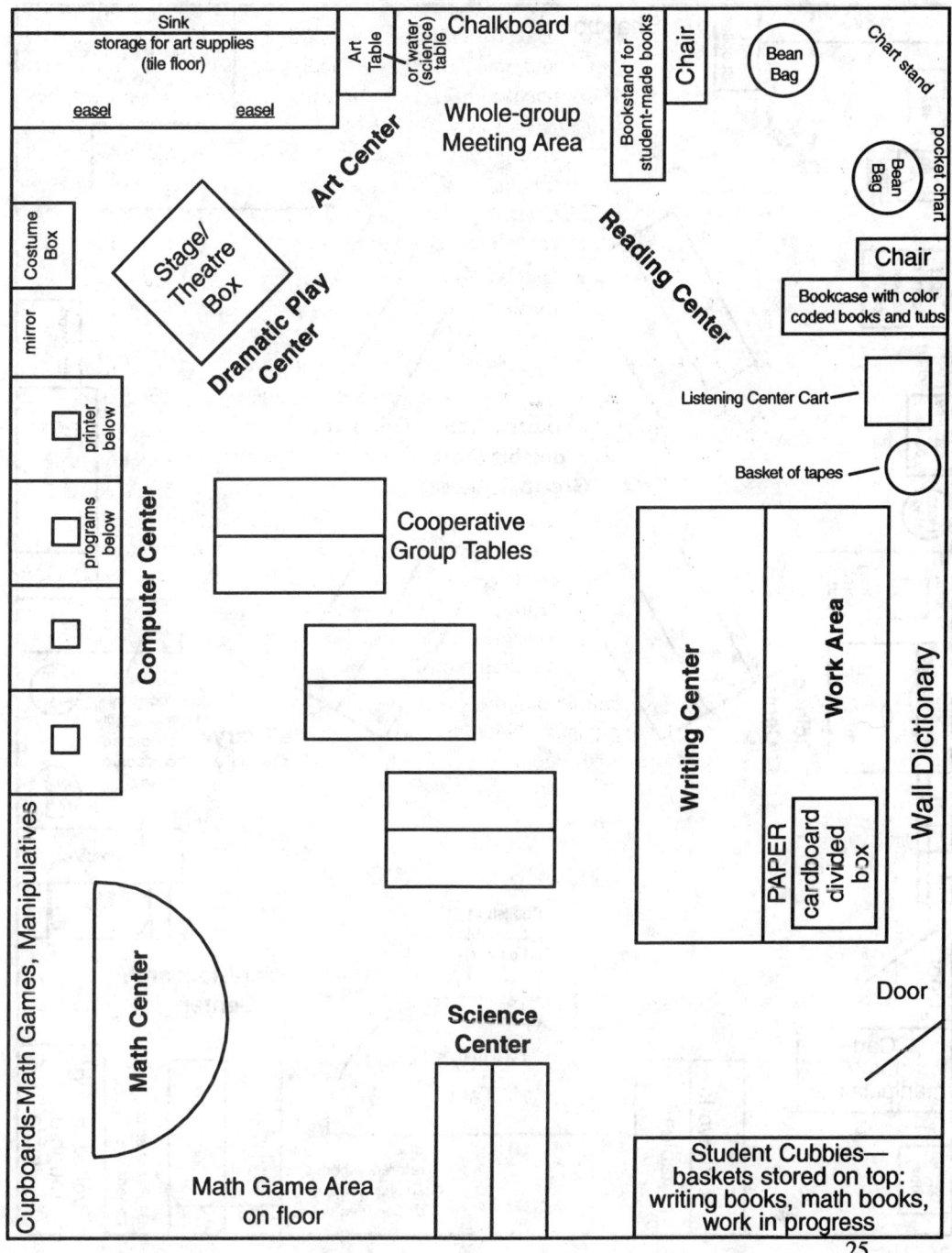

25

Learning Center Classroom Diagram

Grades 4–6

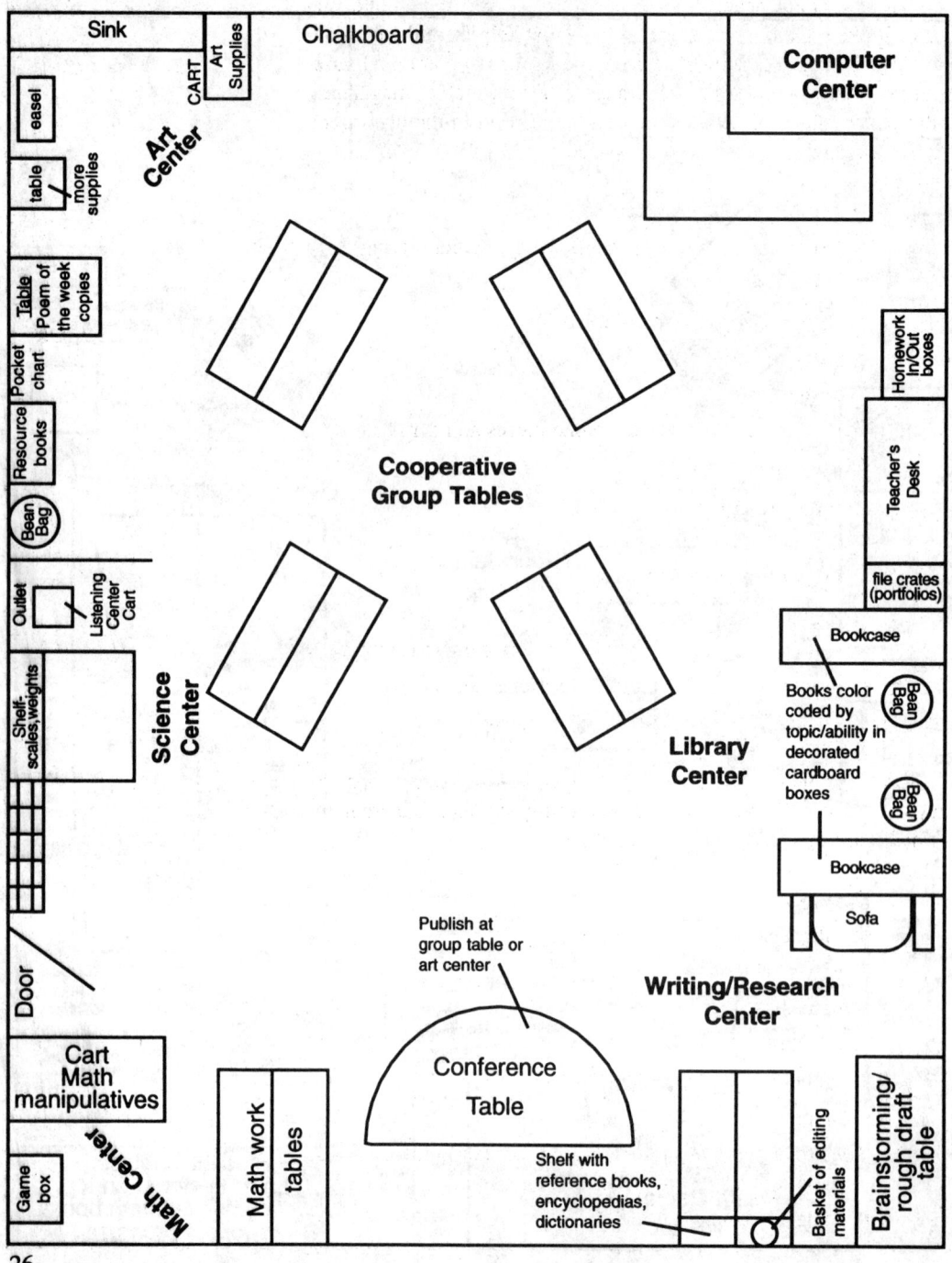

Collecting Manipulatives and Supplies

Learning centers require many manipulatives and supplies, and teachers new to the concept are often overwhelmed at the cost and number of supplies necessary. The best advice is to begin collecting early. Make a list of items desired and enlist help from the community. Send a letter to parents asking for donations of common household items that are typically thrown away. Items such as magazines, toilet paper rolls, and coffee cans can all be used in the classroom. More inexpensive or free supplies include:

- egg cartons (pencil/scissors storage)
- buttons, bottle caps, beans (sorting and classifying)
- plastic bags (book set storage)
- baby food jars (paint or paste)
- hangers (paint drying)
- frozen juice/soup cans (pencil/supply holders)
- margarine tubs and lids (game pieces and cards)
- old magazines for pictures
- fabric scraps for art projects
- old game pieces
- brown lunch bags (puppets)
- sponges (painting)
- cardboard and shoe boxes (table dividers and storage)
- dress-up clothes and jewelry (drama center)
- kitchen/store supplies (drama center)

Besides basic materials like writing paper, colored paper, pencils, crayons, markers, glue, and paint, more costly supplies that are helpful in a learning center classroom include:

- books
- magazines
- newspapers
- games
- puzzles
- globe
- maps
- math manipulatives (building blocks, unifix cubes, pattern blocks, bear counters, dice)
- scales, balances

- magnets
- magnifying glasses
- tape recorder, head sets, blank tapes
- clocks
- calculators
- play money
- measuring cups
- computers
- software

Keep in mind that the more materials available to students, the greater the chance that they will become attracted to learning (Thomas, 1975).

Capitalizing on Human Resources

The need for additional assistance in any classroom is paramount. Teachers need help! Whether it be working with a group of students, putting up a display board, or preparing a handout, help is greatly appreciated. However, the demands on today's parents have limited their time and ability to assist; likewise, limited funds have decreased the availability of paid assistants. Therefore, many teachers are going to extreme measures to obtain and train parent volunteers, paid instructional assistants, and tutors. Strategies include sending frequent requests for help to parents, calling and accepting any time a parent is available to help, training volunteers during lunch recess, teaming with teachers to share assistant time, financing paid help through alternative funds, and working with teachers at other grade levels to establish beneficial tutor schedules, guidelines, and training. Regardless of the resources available, make the best of what is provided. Keep in mind that extra adult help is not mandatory; many learning center classrooms are highly successful with only the teacher in the room. However, be flexible with daily schedules and try to capitalize on whatever is possible. When it comes to children, there can never be too many teachers!

Using Mini-Lessons

It is important that students learn basic guidelines for learning centers before beginning. Topics include:

- Reading the schedule
- Understanding the chart for where students should be
- Rotating through centers
- Working the tape recorder

> **Send a letter to parents asking for donations of common household items that are typically thrown away.**

- Using materials
- Logging work
- Making choices

Students can learn the expectations and procedures via mini-lessons (Opitz, 1994). However, try not to overwhelm them with everything at once. Remember that learning is more successful if it relates to personal experience. Therefore, be brief. List your expectations and combine a few into one mini-lesson. Then, let students experience the centers before reviewing the guidelines again. Repeat this procedure frequently, as new topics and expectations are needed. One learning center classroom has class officers who hold brief, ten-minute meetings each afternoon. In the discussions, students share what is going well and discuss ways to improve things that are not. This approach is a nice way of letting the students share successes, have ownership of some management necessities, and solve relevant problems. It is interesting to note that the most frequent topics involve these mini-lesson ideas.

> **One learning center classroom has class officers who hold brief, ten-minute meetings each afternoon.**

Types of Centers

There are many types of centers that you can create for your students A list of possibilities follows. However, after you have been using centers in yur classroom, you will naturally think of new and exciting centers to begin with your students. Your own unique interests, as well as those of your students, will spark new center ideas constantly.

- Reading Center
- Writing Center
- Listening Center
- Computer Center
- Games and Puzzles Center
- Math Center
- Science Center
- Seasonal Center
- Research Center
- Art Center
- Drama Center
- Social Studies Center
- Hands-On Center

Concluding Remarks

As this chapter opened, you were asked to explore your feelings on learning: how do children learn best, what is important for them to learn, and what is your role in their learning process? Too often in the educational process, the emphasis is placed on teaching rather than learning; as a result, classrooms become teacher-directed rather than student-centered. A learning center classroom provides a wonderful environment for learning. It rewards diversity, encourages creativity, and, most importantly, values each individual as unique. Initiating learning centers is not easy, but the rewards make the process very worthwhile.

Planning Activities

The First Year
The most difficult time to develop learning center activities is during the first year of use (Pfau & Zeddun, 1995). Determining appropriate activities, accumulating supplies, and designing learning centers is extremely time consuming. This is the reason that it was so strongly suggested in Getting Started that teachers new to learning centers begin with a modified approach and gradually add new centers and activities. It is much better to do a good job with only a few centers than to overextend and provide less meaningful experiences for students.

Points to Remember
There are many factors to consider when planning learning center activities. The purpose, objective, and assessment measures must all relate to the activities. In addition, centers must be developmentally appropriate and respect multiple intelligences. They should provide opportunities for student choice, be integrated and fun, and, most importantly, provide hands-on experiences.

Determine the Objective
Objectives are a vital component of instruction because they provide

> Objectives are a vital component of instruction because they provide all members of the learning community with a roadway to success.

all members of the learning community with a roadway to success. Without them, teachers would not have long-term goals for students; in turn, parents would not be able to assist in the educational progress of their children. Expectations would be sadly lacking. If learning centers are used as a vehicle for educational progress, they need clear objectives. Consequently, when planning learning center activities the teacher must consider both purpose and objectives so activities can be designed to meet student needs. If a center is simply a way to occupy student time, the opportunity to educate is wasted.

First, consider what you want students to learn at a particular center. Then, formulate a specific objective and decide how many activities will be used to meet the objective (Opitz, 1994). A planning sheet for a first grade learning center might look like this:

> **If learning centers are used as a vehicle for educational progress, they need clear and relevant objectives.**

Center: "It's About Time"

Purpose: Reinforcement

Objective: to strengthen time-telling skills

Activities:

1. Make "Family Time" mini books using the starter "At _____ o'clock, we _____." on each page.
2. Make paper plate clocks.
3. Listen to *The Grouchy Ladybug* (Carle, 1977) using hand-made clocks to follow along.
4. Play Telling Time Bingo.
5. In math books, use rubber stamp clocks to show the listed times.

Assessment: Teacher observation of student progress and participation/Math book clock problems/Student self-evaluations

Consider Assessment

Though the chapter entitled Authentic Assessment will provide many ideas for assessing student work in learning centers, it is extremely important to remember assessment when planning center activities. In a learning center classroom, there are many activities occurring at once. The teacher must have clear plans as to how progress will be noted and recorded. Each center should have at least one assessment strategy built in; this will help with decisions about student learning and assist the students in becoming responsible, self-evaluators aware of an educational purpose.

Plan Developmentally-Appropriate Activities

The phrase "developmentally appropriate" means that each child's unique progress and growth are used to determine what he or she is ready to accomplish. This philosophy recognizes that students learn at different rates, just as they crawl, walk, and ride a bike at different rates. Children cannot be held to the same expectations or time constraints (McClay, 1996). They must each be regarded as an individual with a unique personality, family background, and set of experiences (D. Ulrey & J. Ulrey, personal communication, March 26, 1993).

Learning centers provide an opportunity to individualize the curriculum with developmentally-appropriate activities. Consider the following goals of developmental education when planning learning center activities for individual students (Province of British Columbia Ministry of Education, 1991):

- Aesthetic and artistic development
- Emotional and social development
- Intellectual development
- Physical development and well-being
- Social responsibility

> **Learning centers provide an opportunity to individualize the curriculum with developmentally-appropriate activities.**

Respect Multiple Intelligences

Current research by Howard Gardner (1985) has illuminated seven different intelligences within each human being:

- Linguistic
- Logical-mathematical
- Spatial
- Bodily-kinesthetic
- Musical
- Interpersonal
- Intrapersonal

Each individual possesses all seven in varying degrees, with certain ones dominant over others. Traditionally, teaching has been directed to the linguistic and logical-mathematical intelligences, minimizing or completely ignoring the additional five (Gardner, 1985). Unfortunately, students who excelled in spatial, bodily-kinesthetic, musical, interpersonal, or intrapersonal intelligence were often labeled slow learners because the teacher did not focus on or even acknowledge those areas of intelligence. What we now know, however, is that students become actively engaged in learning and increase their self-esteem when teaching is directed to one of their dominant intelligences (Garner, 1985). Thus, teachers must attempt to recognize each child's dominant areas and provide experiences that coincide. Teacher Created Materials' *Early Childhood Assessment* (Jasmine, 1995) has observation-based assessments for each of the seven intelligences. The book also provides parent observations for each of the areas. Both can assist teachers in designing learning centers that develop each intelligence within students, as well as activities that are individualized to provide the best possible learning experience for each student.

Provide Opportunities for Student Choice

As discussed in the last chapter, there are many ways to provide students with choices in learning centers. Perhaps the most common in early primary classrooms is to allow students the choice of where and with whom to work. This is done by using a pocket chart with pictures or words to show the center options. Students simply place their name card, picture, craft stick, clothespin, or similar item by the center in which they are going to work.

Another option for student choice used a great deal in upper grade classrooms rests on the belief that, "children tend to forget learning experiences which they have not helped to organize" (Thomas, 1975, p. 262). Letting students plan and organize their own projects is easily incorporated into learning centers. Creating a Project Center has been effective for many teachers, as students can create their own project, experiment, or investigate. The teacher, acting as a resource, can assist each student in choosing an appropriate way of learning and reporting the information.

Teachers have also found success with providing student choice in open subject centers. In these centers, students rotate through math, reading, and writing centers where they enjoy the freedom to work independently or with peers at each location. An eight-year-old student brought a self-selected project to the math station one day. A copy of her note is included on the following page.

> Dear Mrs. M,
> I want to know how many hours old my grandma is. She was born on Aug 19, 1941 at 9:00 PM. Can I work this in class? Maybe we could all figure our age in hours
>
>
>
> love,
> Courtney

> Dear grup,
> I think we shud reserch poler bers. Taylors dad siad thay are the most dangerus animls in the hol world. Wud you like to find owt.
>
> From,
> Jennifer

> **Regardless of the approach to structuring learning centers, allowing for student choice is imperative.**

Regardless of the approach to structuring learning centers, allowing for student choice is imperative. In order for learning to be meaningful and relevant, students must have an interest in the activity and, preferably, ownership.

Plan Integrated Activities

Integrating the curriculum is a way to make learning meaningful and exciting for students, yet is an extremely difficult task (Routman, 1991). The ideal approach is to integrate the curriculum across all subject areas to facilitate meaning in teaching and learning. As illustrated by the planning web on the following page, an integrated curriculum is easily accomplished with learning centers. A primary sample for the ever popular *Brown Bear, Brown Bear, What Do You See?* (Martin, 1983) is on page 37, as well. Both samples provide a basis for integration. The web allows the teacher to integrate a theme across all subject areas. The primary sample uses a piece of literature to incorporate many areas of the curriculum with inviting activities.

Integration Web

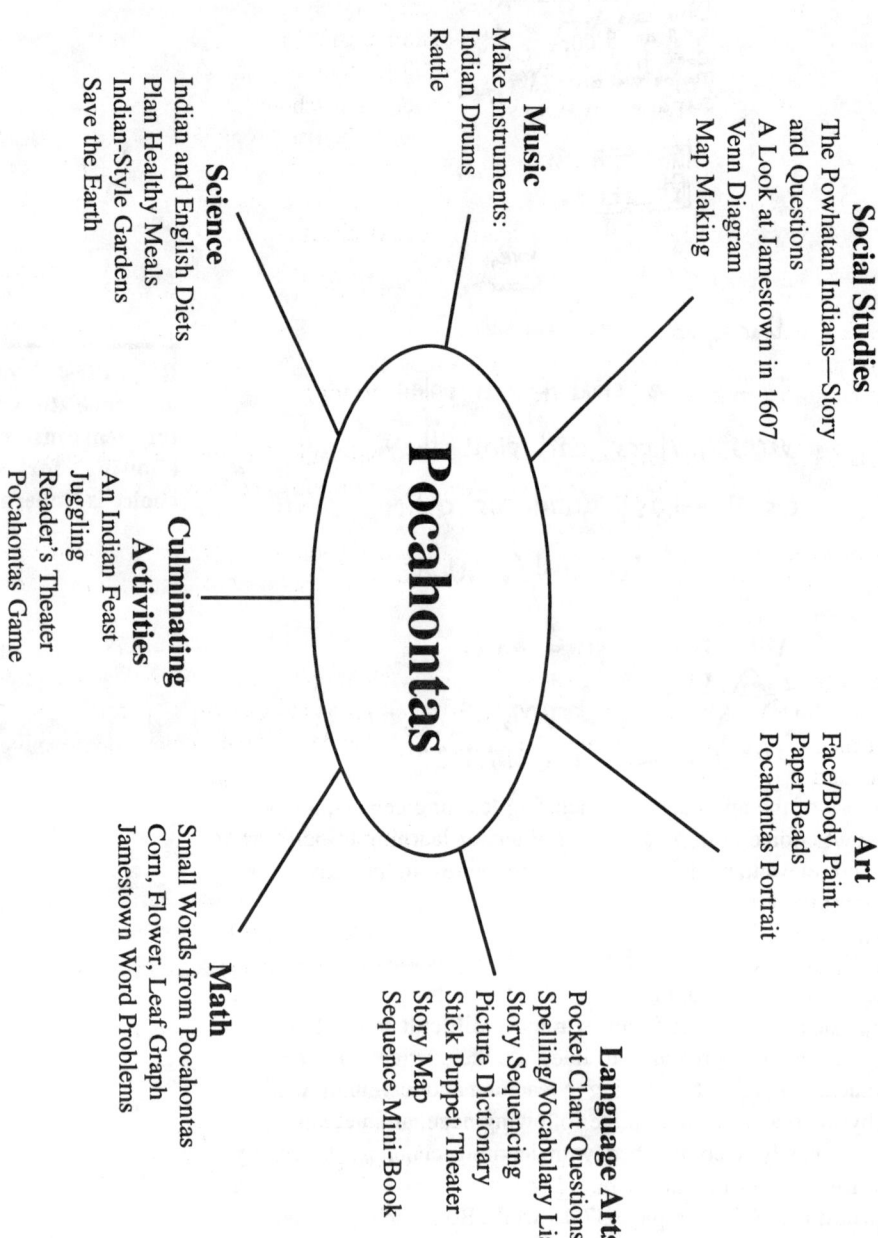

Social Studies
The Powhatan Indians—Story and Questions
A Look at Jamestown in 1607
Venn Diagram
Map Making

Music
Make Instruments:
Indian Drums
Rattle

Science
Indian and English Diets
Plan Healthy Meals
Indian-Style Gardens
Save the Earth

Culminating Activities
An Indian Feast
Juggling
Reader's Theater
Pocahontas Game

Math
Small Words from Pocahontas
Corn, Flower, Leaf Graph
Jamestown Word Problems

Language Arts
Pocket Chart Questions
Spelling/Vocabulary Lists
Story Sequencing
Picture Dictionary
Stick Puppet Theater
Story Map
Sequence Mini-Book

Art
Face/Body Paint
Paper Beads
Pocahontas Portrait

Reprinted from TCM 769 Pocahontas Literature Unit, *Teacher Created Materials, 1995*

Learning Centers

Reading Center: Keep copies of books, poems, and songs at this center for children to read independently. Children may use the flannel board patterns, stick puppets, and sentence strips to retell the story. Make several extra copies of My Little Book of Colors. Since the children will be taking their little books home, you'll still have copies at school for them to read. Keep your list of words that begin with "b" posted here and add to the list throughout the year. (Another list may be made for words that end with "b.") The list of words that rhyme with "bears" may also be posted here. On a bear pattern, make a sign that says, "Have you read these 'beary' good books?" and post the sign near your collection of books about bears.

Writing Center: Children may write their own versions of the story, following the same pattern but inserting their own choices of color words and animal words. Make five-page booklets from white typing paper for this purpose. A story frame may be made for the children, with blanks for color and animal words, or children may do all of the printing.

Math Center: Put several small plastic bears in your estimating jar. Put ten small plastic bears in a jar of the same size and shape to give children a point of reference for their estimates.

Use plastic bears in three colors and sizes for sorting and patterning practice. As an alternative, use the flannel board patterns to make several of each story character to use in similar sorting and patterning activities.

Science Center: Create a Color Detective Center for children to explore colors. With adult supervision, have children come to this center in small groups to use eye droppers to put a few drops of food coloring into small plastic jars of water. Guide children to mix red and yellow, red and blue, and yellow and blue.

Provide several informational books and posters about real bears for your students at this center.

Art Center: Children may work at the easel to paint their own colorful animals. These animals may be displayed on a bulletin board with the caption, BROWN BEAR, BROWN BEAR, WHAT DO YOU SEE? Children (or an adult) may write sentences on each page, following the pattern of the book. These pages (paintings with text) can be made into a class book.

Block Center: Put up and label pictures of animal homes to correspond with the animals in *Brown Bear, Brown Bear, What Do You See?* You may include a barn, birdhouse, cave, doghouse, pond, house, and fishbowl. Children can build these homes, using suitable materials.

Reprinted from TCM 206 Whole Language Units for Predictable Books, *Teacher Created Materials, 1995*

Provide Hands-On Experiences

The most important ingredient of a learning center classroom is hands-on learning. Research by Jean Piaget shows that it is not until children are between ages six and nine that they begin to think abstractly. Rather than just listening, younger children learn much more by touching, smelling, seeing, and tasting (Kantrowitz & Wingert, 1989). Therefore, it is vital to provide students with a wealth of opportunities to touch, smell, see, and taste. Let them manipulate objects, explore freely, and arrive at conclusions that are meaningful to them.

An exciting hands-on science center can be found on pages 39 and 40. This particular sample is from Teacher Created Materials' *Learning Centers Through the Year* (Wallace, 1993), an excellent resource for learning center activities.

Liquid Measurement

Purpose

By filling containers and pouring water from one container into another, the child will learn to associate an amount and size with the words cup, pint, quart, and gallon. Children will also begin to experiment with how many of one container will fill another.

Materials

- Containers: cup, pint, quart, gallon
- Liquid Measurement Chart (page 40)
- Pitcher
- Water
- Paper towels

Preparation

Prepare the Liquid Measurement Chart. Laminate to waterproof it.

Instructions

Children should first take the pitcher to the sink, fill it with water, and then fill and experiment with the containers provided.

Cleanup

Empty all the containers at the sink. Use paper towels to dry off the containers. Also, wipe up any excess water that may have spilled at the center table. Recycle the towels and set all containers on the center table. Children should try to remember answers to each question. They may be asked to demonstrate and share answers.

Helpful Hints

This learning center should be positioned close to the sink.

The teacher could use household items that are the approximate size for the containers. It works best to provide plastic containers that are clear so that the learner can see if the container is full. If the containers being used at the center are not already marked, label each with the appropriate word: cup, pint, quart, gallon.

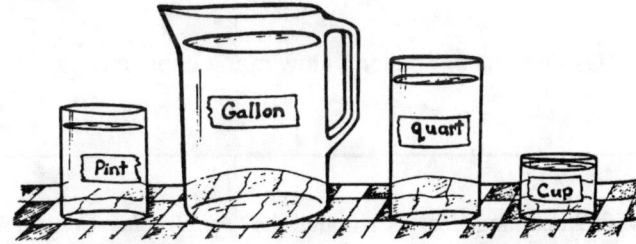

Reprinted from TCM 059 Learning Centers Through the Year, *Teacher Created Materials, 1993*

Liquid Measurement Chart

Look at the chart and try to answer each of the questions.

1. Find the cup. Use it to fill the pint. How many cups in a pint?

2. Find the pint. Use it to fill the quart. How many pints in a quart?

3. Find the quart. Use it to fill the gallon. How many quarts in a gallon?

4. Find the cup. Use it to fill the quart. How many cups in a quart?

5. Find the pint. Use it to fill the gallon. How many pints in a gallon?

6. Find the cup. Use it to fill the gallon. How many cups in a gallon?

Reprinted from TCM 059 Learning Centers Through the Year, *Teacher Created Materials, 1993*

Utilize Technology

Computers offer unlimited learning center opportunities for students. They can be a vital part of an active teaching-learning environment, but they should not be overused or misused. To ensure student interest and energy, computers should be used sparingly, and programs must involve student interaction. Ideas for incorporating computers in a learning classroom include:

- Individual stations with interactive programs and CD-ROMs such as *Oregon Trail* (MECC), *Reader Rabbit* (The Learning Company), *Math Blaster* (Davidson), *Smart Books* (Scholastic), *Word Attack* (Scholastic), *Where in the World is Carmen Sandiego?* (Borderbund), *Word Munchers* (MECC), *ReadingMaze* (Great Wave Software), *EasyBook* (Sunburst), and *KidWorks 2* (Davidson).
- Pods—a few computers networked (local network such as Apple Talk is fine) so students can communicate with each other in story writing and editing
- Station that has access to *Prodigy, America Online, Compuserve,* or other internet capabilities.
- Stations for free writing, journal writing, and language experience stories
- Overhead projection for directions, examples, learning center rotations, etc.

Computers offer unlimited learning center opportunities for students.

Make Learning Fun

This concept is simple. Learning should be fun! No one likes to do something that is a burden, chore, or worse, boring. Even as adults, we whine and gripe at those dreaded tasks of cleaning the house or running errands. Similarly, we often do not like to read a book if it is "required." As unique individuals, adults, like children, enjoy reading materials and learning experiences that are of interest. Hence, try to capture student interests with exciting activities. Encourage children to share and laugh. Though this can be difficult and time consuming to set up, remember, if students are actively involved in an integrated curriculum that is developmentally appropriate and rich in hands-on experiences, the smiles and rewards forthcoming are endless. They will want to work right through recess!

Concluding Remarks

Planning and implementing activities for learning centers can appear overwhelming at first glance, but a systematic approach will make the task easier. Determine instructional goals and objectives, consider assessment strategies, and think about the multiple intelligences of your students. Then, plan activities that will meet individual needs, curriculum requirements, and the hands-on, developmentally-appropriate components of an active learning center classroom. Strive to integrate curriculum in an environment structured to facilitate the needs of each student.

Classroom Management

Getting Started

It is helpful to remember that a new approach for you is also new for your students. Therefore, do not expect perfection when learning centers are first started. It takes time for the teacher and students to adjust to this new format. Keep in mind that you will most likely adapt the organization and management of learning centers several times before arriving at the best format.

When making the transition to learning centers, many teachers suggest sharing the goals with students and involving them in the evaluation process. Explain the reasons for beginning and changing learning centers. Allow students a role in the development of learning centers. This will affirm the presence and importance of learning centers in the classroom, and it will also provide an opportunity to gain valuable insight into student feelings about the instructional transition.

Setting Expectations

Students thrive when the best is expected of them, and they work hard to meet challenges that are within their reach. However, if students are overwhelmed by too many expectations, they can become

> **When making the transition to learning centers, many teachers suggest sharing the goals with students and involving them in the evaluation process.**

frustrated, show anxiety, and exhibit behavior problems (Thomas, 1975). Consequently, it benefits all participants to begin slowly and gradually increase the requirements. For example, the goal for the first week can be to simply understand the schedule and rotation. The activities should be easy, familiar tasks, allowing students an opportunity to experience centers and gain an understanding of the approach. The next week, focus can include following directions, increasing the activity levels, and providing only a little assistance when students are getting started. Requiring them to read and re-read the directions will better prepare them for a learning center environment. Students need to become independent, responsible individuals. Focusing on the importance of reading directions in the beginning of learning center implementation will assist all students in assuming their roles as active learners.

Positive Reinforcement

Most everyone agrees that when students feel good about themselves they are more likely to succeed. Crucial to the learning center philosophy is that students take an active part in their education, experimenting, exploring, and creating knowledge that is meaningful and relevant to their lives. In order to do this, students must feel comfortable in the environment and confident that their ventures will be respected and valued. They must believe that their work and behavior will not be criticized, negated, or made fun of. Thus, the teacher must gain children's trust so that they feel comfortable about taking risks and venturing into unfamilar territory. The most thoughtful way to do this is through positive reinforcement, a philosophy of management that focuses on the positive things that students are doing instead of the negative. It is not uncommon in education to find teachers who pay most attention to the negative aspects of student behavior and accomplishments.

> "Jimmy, why haven't you finished your math assignment?"

> "Diane, please pay attention."

> "If you do not get to work immediately, Tommy, I will have to send a note home."

Unfortunately, these types of comments are frequently heard in classrooms. Because teachers are responsible for so many students, those acting inappropriately tend to stand out and receive attention. Positive reinforcement, however, recognizes the work of students behaving appropriately and attempts to commend them while improving the actions of others. For example, when a child is having difficulty completing his or her work, rather than commenting

> **Because teachers are responsible for so many students, those acting inappropriately tend to stand out and receive attention.**

about the negative behavior, praise another child who is working diligently. Likewise, when students are talking out of turn or disturbing peers, the teacher can comment on students who are waiting their turn and being respectful.

> "Carlos, I really like the way you are standing in line so quietly."

> "You are doing a super job at the writing station, John."

> "I love the way Bryce and Michelle are working together on their story."

This positive approach to discipline usually works amazingly well, particularly with younger students and assists in managing a learning environment where students feel confident and respected. If a negative behavior persists, simply standing next to or sitting with the disruptive child will usually work. Any additional intervention should take place privately.

Center Schedules

The daily schedule is also critical for classroom management. If the teacher or students are constantly interrupted, behavior problems increase and authentic learning decreases. Determining a schedule that is best for your classroom is a difficult task. Take into consideration the amount of time needed for each subject or set of centers, the availability of instructional assistants or volunteers, lunch and recess breaks, special programs like library visits, music/physical education classes, and pull-out programs that remove individual students from the classroom. The following three pages illustrate effective schedules for two learning center classrooms.

Determining a schedule that is best for your classroom is a difficult task.

Sample Schedule
Grades 1–3

8:45–9:00	Welcome, Attendance, Lunch Count, Flag Salute, Calendar
9:00–10:45	Subject Centers: Students are placed in four heterogeneous groups for the day and rotate through four centers: Math, Writing, Reading, and Free Choice
10:45–11:00	Snack/Outdoor Play
11:00–11:55	Theme Centers (Quantity 8): Students are placed in eight groups and complete one center each day. Centers integrate art, writing, problem solving, social studies, reading, computation, spelling, oral language, and cooperative learning.
11:55–12:40	Lunch/Organized Outdoor Games
12:40–1:15	Shared Reading/D.E.A.R. (Drop Everything And Read)
1:15–2:00	Science Lab
2:00–2:45	Monday—Physical Education
	Tuesday—Health
	Wednesday—Music
	Thursday—Library
	Friday—Physical Education

Sample Schedule
Grades 4–6

8:15–8:30　　Opening, Attendance, Lunch Count, Flag Salute, Sharing

8:30–9:30　　Social Studies Centers (two days a week)/Social Studies Whole Group Lesson, Individual Work, or Partner Work (three days a week)

　　　　　　　(1) Computers/GeoSafari/Social Studies Games

　　　　　　　(2) Art Activity

　　　　　　　(3) Writing/Research Assignment

　　　　　　　(4) Reader's Theater—Skit

　　　　　　　(5) Teacher-Directed Lesson (Review concepts)

9:30–9:45　　Mini Grammar Lesson (i.e., common nouns, plural nouns)

9:45–10:30　　Writer's Workshop (students placed in six heterogeneous groups)

　　　　　　　(1) Brainstorming Station (word web)

　　　　　　　(2) First Draft/Peer Edit Station

　　　　　　　(3) Teacher Conference Station

　　　　　　　(4) Second Draft/Cursive Station

　　　　　　　(5) Publishing Station (Computers)

10:30–10:45　　Recess

10:45–11:10　　Problem of the Day (Math) & Journal Writing

(continued on the next page)

Sample Schedule *(cont.)*

11:10–11:55 Math Centers (three days a week)/Whole Group Directed Lesson (one day per week)/Independent Work (one day per week)

   (1) Computers

   (2) Logic Sheets/Puzzlers

   (3) Geoboards/Calculators

   (4) Flash Cards/Multiplication Bingo/Fraction Games/Time with Clocks/Money Activities with Cash Drawer

   (5) Teacher-Directed Group

12:00–12:45 Lunch/Outdoor Games

12:45–1:00 Daily Oral Language

1:00–1:20 Core Literature—In small groups, students take turns reading from a core literature book the teacher has chosen (followed by short discussion).

1:20–2:10 Shared Reading/Whole Group Lesson/Reader's Workshop

   (1) Reader's Theater—skits

   (2) Poetry (read, re-write, create)

   (3) Guided Reading with the Teacher

   (4) Illustrating Student-Made Books

   (5) Independent Silent Reading

2:10–2:30 Science Centers (two days per week)/Science Lab (one day per week)/Physical Education (two days per week)

   (1) Discovery Center

   (2) Hands-On Activity

   (3) Art/Illustrations

Management Strategies

Because students work at a variety of locations and on numerous activities with little teacher direction, the organization and management skills needed are numerous. In addition to setting expectations, using positive reinforcement and scheduling the day, there are many more hints that help the teacher manage an effective learning center classroom. Consider the following when implementing centers:

- ◆ General Classroom Rules
- ◆ Acceptable Noise Level
- ◆ Location and Rotation Chart
- ◆ Limiting Center Numbers
- ◆ Monitoring Choices
- ◆ Introducing New Centers
- ◆ Changing Activities
- ◆ Managing Materials
- ◆ Using Equipment
- ◆ Finish-Up Time
- ◆ Special Needs Students

General Classroom Rules

There are initial rules that need to be established and understood prior to using learning centers. Though learning center classrooms provide students the freedom to learn independently, there must be a balance between freedom and order (Thomas, 1975). Try to state the rules in a positive manner as in the following example:

- ◆ Show respect for your teacher, peers, and materials.
- ◆ Try your hardest in everything you do.
- ◆ Ask questions to three classmates before the teacher.
- ◆ Work cooperatively to solve problems.

General rules may have to be amended as new situations arise. Review the rules frequently, using a discussion format so that students gain a better understanding of the reasons behind each rule (Thomas, 1975). Ask students, "Why should we work cooperatively to solve problems?" Guide them in discovering that cooperation helps all participants by providing multiple ideas and solutions.

Acceptable Noise Level

Keep in mind that the noise level in a learning center classroom is often higher than in a traditional setting. In a learning center envi-

> **There are initial rules that need to be established and understood prior to using learning centers.**

ronment, students are actively learning, and communication is vital. It is expected that students brainstorm, share, and report findings with classmates. Thus, the noise level can elevate at times. It is helpful to develop a signal that indicates the necessity for quieter voices. Perhaps a flash of the lights, a chord on the piano, or a "pass the word" approach will work for you.

Location and Rotation Chart

Many teachers suggest using a chart or board to show where each student is working. Though this will vary, depending on the types of centers and groups used, it is invaluable for knowing exactly where each child is supposed to be. For an "open" model, where students choose their centers, a peg board or clothespin chart is perfect. Simply make a tag of some sort for each child and have the class place their name tags by the center in which they are working. If students rotate through centers in assigned groups, a chart or cards can be made with group member names and locations.

> **Many teachers suggest using a chart or board to show where each student is working.**

Center #1	Center #2	Center #3	Center #4
Red Group	Blue Group	Yellow Group	Green Group
Bob	Susie	Julie	Joelle
Cindy	Phillip	Nicholas	Grant
Alex	Adam	Dean	Loretta
Paul	Susan	Tracy	Jo
Tyler	Hanna	Whitney	Emily
Haley	Aaron	Jacob	Allison
Katie	Megan		John

This chart is easy to use as a rotation chart, also, as the center numbers on the top can simply be moved as each group rotates. If classroom computers are available, there are also several professional programs that allow students to access personal portfolios and rotation charts.

Limiting Center Numbers

Certain centers may be more meaningful if fewer students are working at the same time; on the other hand, some centers may require more students in order to facilitate the learning. A Center Chart accommodates this, displaying which centers are open and how many students may work at each. This type of sign is easily made and can apply to pre-primary students, using actual photographs to display which centers are available, and for more advanced students, using center titles and specifics. It is also possible to limit the number of people at each center by placing a number on a chart by each center of how many people may be there or by having only that number of hooks or places for names.

Another option is to have the maximum or desired number of students placed on each center's location sign and ask children to place their names, clothespins, or similar items at the actual center (Pattillo & Vaughan, 1992).

Monitoring Choices

There are times when it is advisable to monitor the choices students are making. For instance, if the teacher allows students to choose which centers to work in and a particular child works at the same center each day or avoids another center, the teacher must give guidance and implement a program that allows the student choices, yet requires participation at all centers. There are two common ways that this may be done. First, students can have a Center Recording Sheet, like the sample on page 53. On this form, the teacher or students record centers as they are completed. The sheet is attached to a work folder or packet so that it is easily accessible. The teacher can leave a note or specific directions for one or each student (i.e., "Jason, please work at Center #4 today and do two of the activities.") Second, each student can be given a list or wheel of all the centers and activities for the week. Once students complete an activity at a center, they check it off or color it in to note that it is completed (Pattillo & Vaughan, 1992). A sample for the *Brown Bear, Brown Bear, What Do You See?* (Martin, 1983) activities shown in the previous chapter could look like this:

> **There are times when it is advisable to monitor the choices students are making.**

[Wheel diagram with center labeled "Brown Bear, Brown Bear Week of:" surrounded by six sections: Block Center, Reading Center, Science Center, Math Center, Writing Center, Art Center]

This approach guides students in future decisions, as once all activities at a center are completed, students cannot return to it until the other assigned activities are completed, as well. This method also allows the teacher to quickly get a picture of what activities each child has been working on and/or needs to spend more time on. In addition, the teacher can individualize lists or wheels by crossing certain items off or adding activities to particular student's forms. If students are computer literate, they can keep their center recording sheets on their own personal floppy disks. As they complete each item they get practice with word processing and develop a sense of pride in their accomplishments.

Center Recording Sheet

Name:
Date:
Center Completed:
1.
2.
3.
4.
5.
6.
7.
8.
9.
10.

Reprinted from TCM 059 Learning Centers Through the Year, *Teacher Created Materials, 1993*

Introducing New Centers

It is important to introduce new centers to the entire class before having students visit them. If students are somewhat familiar with the materials and process, fewer management problems will arise. Some teachers suggest presenting a lesson such as a science experiment to the whole class and then placing all of the materials at a center. This provides students with more time to explore and inquire independently, yet they have been acquainted to the materials, methods, and expectations.

Keep in mind, though, that when introducing a new center, it is generally not necessary to present a sample or give the specific directions. It is valuable for students to learn the importance of being creative and reading and re-reading directions. Too often we tell our students exactly what to do, how to do it, and what it should look like. Learning centers provide a safe place for students to think critically, solve their own problems, and be proud of their creativity.

Changing Activities

When and how activities are changed depends on the structure of the learning centers environment. If you use centers each day and require all students to rotate through each one, new activities will be needed on a daily basis. If students are grouped for a week or longer and asked to complete one center per day, activities will not need to be added or changed until each group has rotated through all of the centers. Regardless, once learning centers are up and running, it becomes easier to add activities on an ongoing basis.

It is also nice to incorporate special days or school celebrations when desired. For instance, on the one-hundredth day of school, it may be beneficial to read *The Wolf's Chicken Stew* (Kasza, 1987) and introduce a 100th Day Center. Sample task cards for this center can be found on the following page. Allowing students to explore and complete one or all of the activities will be an enjoyable, hands-on center that stimulates creativity while building mathematical concepts.

> **It is important to introduce new centers to the entire class before having students visit them.**

100th Day Activity Cards

Cut apart these cards to use in centers on your 100th Day Celebration!

Draw what you think you will look like when you are 100 years old.	Make a list of five things you have 100 of at home.
Estimate how far 100 steps would take you from where you are right now. Check your guess!	Which of these three jars has 100 beans in it?
Name ten things that there are 100 of in the classroom.	Count the 100 creatures or things that are pictured in one of the books on this table.
How many people do you think 100 kernels of unpopped popcorn can feed? After you make your guess, pop 100 kernels with adult supervision.	Could you eat 100 pancakes at one time? Name three things you could eat 100 of at one time!

Reprinted from TCM 342 Connecting Math & Literature, *Teacher Created Materials, 1991*

Managing Materials

Learning centers facilitate a sense of community; individuals become part of a whole, taking responsibility for each other and their environment. The process of establishing a system to manage materials and supplies can be complex as well as time consuming; however, once the learning center classroom is organized, maintenance is simple (Pfau & Zeddun, 1995), as students know where materials belong and assume responsibility for cleaning up after they are finished with center activities.

It may be useful to list all of the materials needed for each center on the directions. Students can plan ahead by reading what they need and making sure each item is available. This also helps during cleanup.

> It may be useful to list all of the materials needed for each center on the directions.

Shelves, supply carts, boxes, and manila envelopes can all be used to store center materials. The art center, for instance, may have a supply cart with creative materials. The reading corner can be made of bookshelves, color-coded baskets for book levels, and cardboard boxes covered in contact paper. Boxes can also be used to hold student work folders and files. Manila envelopes can be laminated to hold small games or puzzles. It is helpful to attach a title and direction card before laminating.

For student supplies, some teachers suggest that each child be given a shoe box to store pencils, crayons, and like items. This way, when students move from one center to another, they simply take their boxes with them (Poppe & Van Matre, 1985).

Regardless of the materials used and the storage space available, it is imperative that items be clearly labeled, accessible to students, and presented in an organized fashion. That is, math materials should be located together and not dispersed throughout the room. Likewise, students in the Listening Center should not have to travel a great distance or search the room for story tapes. Planning ahead and organizing materials can make an enormous difference in classroom management. When items students need are carefully organized, disruptions can be kept to a minimum.

Using Equipment

Students cannot be expected to know how to use all of the equipment in a learning center classroom. Tape recorders, overhead projectors, microscopes, and computers can all be used by students if they are properly maintained, labeled, and introduced. While the equipment options vary, it is important to remember that those chosen must be safe for students to use. Consider who will be responsible for plugging/unplugging items and moving them to other locations. Be careful that students are aware of safety issues. As the teacher, monitor student use of equipment at all times. Additional management strategies include marking the volume level and color coding important buttons on the tape recorder, as well as teaching students how to turn on, save work, and turn off computers.

Finish-Up Time
If you select the open approach, where students move on to another center when they are finished with one, you will not need to schedule time to allow students to finish uncompleted activities. However, if you have a scheduled rotation time, great thought and effort needs to be dedicated to the task of allowing students ample time to complete activities and assignments at an individualized pace. It is unfair to assume or expect that all students will finish within the same amount of time. The most common way to do this is to provide a small amount of time each day, usually fifteen to twenty minutes, when students can work on unfinished activities. Those who are finished can make great use of the time in the reading corner. Another option is to provide a longer period of time, such as one hour, at the end of the week. Students who are finished enjoy more time to explore in centers of their choice. A chart of Things to Do can also remind students of options available when work is completed. Nevertheless, each student will need a place to store unfinished work. Though many teachers simply use a central location, such as a box labeled Unfinished Work, personal experience has found this method highly unorganized for student use. A personal location, such as a folder or portfolio for each child, saves time in passing out work and serves students with a constant reminder of what needs to be finished.

> **Students who are finished enjoy more time to explore in centers of their choice.**

Rushing to Complete Work
Most teachers new to learning centers experience problems with students rushing to complete their work, especially if the free-choice activities available to those who are finished with their work are appealing. First of all, knowing that this is a natural phenomena will ease frustrations for the teacher. Students new to the approach are often astounded by the freedom and seek to use it more as play. They hurry through their tasks, doing sloppy, incorrect work. However, after they realize that the freedom with learning centers provides the time to do quality work, they usually slow down and begin taking more time on their projects. Unfortunately, this is not an overnight revelation. It takes time, positive reinforcement, and modeling by the teacher. Steps to help include:

- Insist on quality work. If a student has rushed through a task and done a poor job, ask that it be redone.
- Praise students for taking their time and doing a "quality job." Share quality work with the class.
- Do not allow students to rotate until a specified time has elapsed.
- Introduce more advanced concepts, such as the five elements of a story and book reports to primary students and research projects and the scientific method to upper grade students.
- Model the process for the class and ask each student to incorporate the concept into learning center work.

What About the Child with Special Needs?

Many teachers are overwhelmed with special needs students. The number of attention deficit disorder, attention deficit hyperactivity disorder, fetal alcohol syndrome, and inclusion students is rising dramatically, and teachers are faced with finding ways to accommodate a diverse group of students within one classroom. In addition, issues of English language acquisition and development contribute to classroom diversity. For most of these special needs students, a learning center environment meets individual needs far better than a traditional setting. Learning centers can be tailored to individual needs, limited attention spans, and specific language needs.

Some students, particularly those with learning disabilities or attention deficit disorder, can have difficulty in a less structured environment (Hallahan & Kauffman, 1994) and are sometimes more successful in settings with greater structure and less stimuli. Hence, for learning disability and attention deficit disorder students who are having problems in the learning center classroom, try providing a cubicle made easily out of a cardboard box. Encourage them to complete learning center activities at the cubicle location. It is important that they choose to do their work in this special location and that they understand why it will help them learn. It is also easy to create a few cubicles for all students to utilize, if desired or to design a few learning centers with three-sided work areas.

Although uncommon, students without learning disabilities or attention deficit disorder can have trouble adapting to learning centers, as well. The freedom and independence provided by the learning center approach can overwhelm some students and lead to problems. In this event, try any or all of the following suggestions:

Encourage them to complete learning center activities at the cubicle location.

- Individualize the student's work. Make daily goals with the child and meet regularly to monitor and evaluate progress.
- Assign the student a buddy to work with at all of the centers.
- Establish a behavior contract with the student and parents. Record behavior and progress on a daily card and send it home for a parent to sign and return each day.
- As a last result, do not allow the student to participate in the centers until the improper behavior is modified. Give him or her the assignments to do at a desk and do not allow movement around the room. Though that is extremely harsh treatment, misbehaving students usually miss the freedom that learning centers allow and change their behavior quickly.

Regardless of the method used to assist students who are experiencing difficulties in the classroom, communicate with parents or guardians on a regular basis. Enlist their support and keep them abreast of student progress. Also, refer students to the Student Study Team, if possible. The input of a team of educators from your site can provide invaluable suggestions and strategies to meet the specific needs of any student having problems in the classroom.

Remember, the transition to learning centers is a new experience for your students, and one that requires time, patience, and trust for everyone involved. An effective classroom is like a large family, a group of people who live and work together toward the same goal. However, establishing this type of climate based on trust and respect is a difficult task, yet one that is crucial for success. One suggestion is to create a "Classroom Family Tree," where each child becomes an apple or leaf on a bulletin board or real life tree. Another way to assist students in becoming more respectful of their peers is to create a large puzzle on a bulletin board entitled "We All Work Together." Give each child a piece of the puzzle and ask the class to decorate their pieces with pictures and write about how they help out in the classroom. You will be surprised how this simple activity can make classroom management easier, as students gain appreciation for others, begin working collectively to solve problems, and exhibit less anxiety and behavior problems. Also, the display makes a constant reminder of expectations and a beautiful bulletin board.

> **Regardless of the method used to assist students who are experiencing difficulties in the classroom, communicate with parents or guardians on a regular basis.**

Concluding Remarks

Effective classroom management strategies are critical in any classroom, especially an active learning center environment. With students of diverse needs and backgrounds working on various activities at many stations, the teacher must have or develop management techniques that promote high expectations, build the student's sense of self, and encourage responsibility. Instructional time is valuable and must be utilized for meaningful learning experiences. Classroom activities such as setup, center rotation, and cleanup should be efficient and take as little time as possible. A learning center classroom provides students with a sense of community, and effective management strategies create feelings of shared responsibility and success.

Student Accountability

How Can Students Be Held Accountable?
With all of the "hustle and bustle" of a learning center classroom, how can the teacher ensure that students complete the necessary centers? How is it possible to know that students are spending quality time at each center and learning from their experiences? Is there a way the teacher can keep track of students' work and hold them responsible for their tasks? These are the most common concerns of teachers new to learning centers. They represent a genuine concern for student learning and are the focus of this chapter.

Work Folders
Weekly or daily work folders are the most common way teachers hold students accountable for their work. These folders are a place for students to store their work in progress. They permit the teacher to look at each child as an individual, taking into consideration learning style, developmental stage, interest, and progress.

- What is Jaime doing in math?
- What is his latest journal entry?
- How does he feel about his work this week?

> **Weekly or daily work folders are the most common way teachers hold students accountable for their work.**

Seeing all of a student's work in one place assists the teacher in assessing each child's development in all areas. In addition, the teacher enjoys the liberty of leaving specific directions for students in the folders or a simple "See Me" sticker on the front. Work folders provide an organized, time-efficient way for work to be stored and easily accessed by both the student and teacher. Most teachers suggest stapling a Center Recording Sheet, Daily Plan, or Weekly Plan to the front of the folder so it is easy to assess student responsibility and choices. A Daily Plan or Weekly Plan cover sheet can list all of the centers open, have a space to write the date each activity is completed, and an area for teacher and parent comments. Because many of the centers will be hands-on experiences that do not have a traditional "ditto" to share learning, it is suggested that these plan sheets be sent home for a parent to sign. This way, the teacher, student, and parent can see which activities are being done and when.

Student Journals

The use of journals has become a popular component in learning center classrooms. Though there are many types of journals used, reflection journals hold students accountable for their learning by asking them to reflect on what they have learned, what they still have questions about, and what they want to know more about (Routman, 1991). In so doing, reflection journals guide students in developing responsibility and self-evaluation skills.

Independent Contracts

Some teachers ask students to decide how they will use their time each day. This approach encourages students to plan ahead; it shares goals with the teacher and parents, and it serves as a contract between the student and teacher. Independent contracts reinforce responsibility by expecting students to achieve the goals they have set.

Goals

Another option is to have students develop weekly, monthly, or semester goals. Using this strategy, each child must meet with the teacher to discuss the expectations they have placed on themselves. Are the goals realistic? Are they challenging? Together, the teacher and student can determine the best course of action. Involving students in this process enlightens the teacher as to each student's perceptions and aspirations and gives ownership and responsibility to the learner. The goals can be placed in a convenient yet private place for each student, perhaps attached to the inside cover of each work folder. This permits students to revisit goals on a regular basis and adjust habits and behaviors, if necessary. Or, students can add more goals if needed. An example follows on the next page.

> Independent contracts reinforce responsibility by expecting students to achieve the goals they have set.

It is also valuable to have students do a written reflection at the end of the time period established for goals. Did they meet their goals? Why or why not? What, if anything, will they do differently next time? What would they like to focus on next time? This process assists students in developing self-evaluation and personal responsibility skills.

```
+------------------------------------------------+
|              My Weekly Goals. . .              |
|                                                |
|  Name_____ Date _____   |
|                                                |
|  My first goal is _____    |
|  _____        |
|                                                |
|  My second goal is _____     |
|  _____        |
|                                                |
|  My third goal is _____     |
|  _____        |
|                                                |
|  My plan to achieve these goals: _____    |
|  _____        |
|  _____        |
|  _____        |
|                                                |
|  _____        _____      |
|  Student Signature       Teacher Signature     |
+------------------------------------------------+
```

> It is also valuable to have students do a written reflection at the end of the time period established for goals.

Student-Led Conferences

Once students are given ownership of their learning experiences and have become involved in the evaluation process, they deserve the opportunity to share their progress. Rather than the teacher explaining the student's goals and growth, many teachers allow students to take credit for their accomplishments through student-led conferences. In this setting, students take charge of the traditional parent/teacher meeting. Primary students play a smaller role, perhaps sharing just one piece of work; whereas, older students can plan and lead the entire conference (Ryan, 1994). A fifth grade teacher has students plan and script the entire conference, taking into consideration pre-determined goals for behavior and learning. Working in conjunction with the teacher and actually rehearsing with peers, students take control of the meeting and accept responsibility for not only completing their learning but evaluating and reporting it, as well.

Concluding Remarks

It is critical that students be held accountable for their work in a learning center classroom. Underlying the open classroom philosophy is that students are unique individuals who deserve an individualized, self-paced, and meaningful education. Learning centers provide this but also require that students take responsibility for their work. If the teacher is constantly checking items, encouraging students to do appropriate activities, and keeping students on task, instructional time is wasted. In contrast, if students learn time-management strategies, play a role in determining projects and goals, and are held accountable for their progress, the teacher is available to facilitate and provide valuable instruction, encouragement, and experiences.

Authentic Assessment

What Is Authentic Assessment?
Traditionally, assessment has come in the form of paper-and-pencil tests that focus on incremental skills and can be graded objectively (Jasmine, 1993). Students have been labeled, retained, and promoted based on their ability to perform on an exam. Unfortunately, these tests are not an ideal assessment tool for any child. While they may help the teacher evaluate his or her planning and teaching strategies, these tests do not accurately measure a student's knowledge or progress. These tests simply demonstrate how a student is doing in comparison to his or her peers (Ryan, 1994). More often than not, testing places the emphasis on competition rather than development of individual talent. As a result, product becomes more important than process. In a competitive environment, teaching has a tendency to become coaching for a test, and real learning and real thinking are undervalued (Neill & Medina, 1989).

> **Students have been labeled, retained, and promoted based on their ability to perform on an exam.**

The preferred approach is that of authentic assessment, which highlights each student's progress over time and focuses on process as well as product. Authentic assessment values approximation; students have a sense of accomplishment for what they have learned rather than a sense of defeat because a product is not perfect.

Strategies used in authentic assessment facilitate comparison of a student's accomplishments with his or her previous work, not the work of classmates, and include information on how the student learns and works. Authentic assessment is essential for planning appropriate learning centers for each child. Items like writing samples and tape recorded reading samples are popular authentic assessments as they allow the student to demonstrate progress and the teacher to gain worthy information about the child's growth. The teacher then has valuable documentation to share with the child and his or her parents.

Can Authentic Assessment Be Used with Centers?
Many teachers fear that assessing student progress will be an extremely difficult task in a classroom where students are actively engaged in learning centers. With students working on multiple activities at a variety of locations, isn't assessment of each student's progress almost an impossible task? The answer is a resounding "NO!" Most teachers find that learning centers provide a perfect environment for authentic assessment. In addition, they find that assessment is easier in an active, learning center classroom than in a traditional environment. The learning center classroom is alive with learning and activity, and opportunities to assess students individually or in small groups are readily available. Teachers using learning centers tend to know more about their students' learning because classroom focus is on each child as an individual rather than all children as a group. Rather than teaching a lesson to thirty students and then giving the same test to each child, the teacher, provided the classroom is structured and organized to maximize student learning, has the opportunity to watch, conference, and understand how each student processes information.

This watching of students provides the teacher with incredible opportunities to assess how students work together and independently (Goodman, 1978). It allows the teacher to truly study the children to learn more about each one as an individual.

Organized Environment
In order to assess students as individuals and spend a great deal of time conferencing and watching, the classroom environment must be structured to accommodate both an individualized assessment approach and maximum learning for all students. If the teacher is busy with pencil sharpening tasks, solving behavioral problems, or talking with a volunteer, valuable instructional and assessment time is wasted; if the teacher is working with one student while the other children are not engaged in learning, time is wasted. However, if the classroom teacher facilitates a structured program where expectations are

> **Most teachers find that learning centers provide a perfect environment for authentic assessment.**

clear and students are actively learning, the opportunities for assessment are almost unlimited.

Examples of Assessment

Perhaps the easiest way to show growth in written language is through the display of actual student work. Writing journals provide clear evidence of student progress and require very little teacher direction. Samples from a student's writing journal can be found below.

This particular teacher has the student choose several entries to place in his or her portfolio when the journal is complete. A key point to remember, however, is that each entry be properly dated. This can be accomplished by simply placing a date stamp at the writing center. It provides the chronological base of development. Teachers also suggest writing notes on the journal entries regarding what is discussed at the student-teacher writing conference. This makes it easy for the teacher, instructional assistant, student, or parent to quickly review the concepts being introduced or reinforced.

Writing journals provide clear evidence of student progress and require very little teacher direction.

> Amanda
> I Want [went] to the Raavrea [river] Woath [with]
> my CoaSa [cousins] for tow [two] Day [days]
> and The neaX [next] Day We Wan't [went]
> to Big Bare [Bear] for noe [one] Day
> and We coe't [caught] SiX fahe [fish]
> and We hae [had] fun.
>
> 9-25-95
>
> Good job! (Lots of "ands" — let's use periods and start new sentences :)

Problem solving and math task samples are also valued components of assessment and are easily used as learning centers. A sample can be found on page 68. Notice that a rubric accompanies the task on page 69 and assists the students in developing self-evaluation skills.

Math Task Sample

Name _____ Date _____

Look at the number sentence below.

$$5-2=3$$

- Make up a story to go with the number sentence.

- Draw a picture to go with your story.

- Take turns telling your story to a partner.

- Be ready to tell your story to me.

- Use the space below to do your work.

Reprinted from TCM 790 Teaching Basic Skills Through Literature: Math, *Teacher Created Materials, 1995*

Math Task Rubric

Score 3: High Pass

The student...

... demonstrates detailed understanding of major concepts.

... draws a picture that clearly illustrates a given equation in both number and operation.

... creates an appropriate story to go with illustrations for the equation as evidenced by an oral telling of the story.

Score 2: Pass

The student...

... demonstrates a general understanding of the major concepts.

... either creates an appropriate story to go with the equation as evidenced by an oral telling of the story or draws a picture that clearly illustrates the equation.

Score 1: Needs Revision

The student...

... demonstrates a lack of skills necessary to reach a solution.

... draws a picture or tells a story that has little or nothing to do with the given equation.

Score 0: No Response

Reprinted from TCM 790 Teaching Basic Skills Through Literature: Math, *Teacher Created Materials, 1995*

Teacher observations are a popular form of authentic assessment, as well. Many teachers make observations on a daily basis in the form of anecdotal records. Some choose to focus on a small group of students each day to ensure that each child has been viewed by the end of the week; others attempt to watch as many as possible during a given day or time period. The sample observation form shown on page 71 is a popular choice among teachers and can be completed while students are engaged in learning centers.

Videotaped samples are also an option. One teacher has tapes for students and records them working, sharing, reading, conferencing, and describing the contents of their portfolios. Students and parents enjoy watching and saving the tapes at the end of the year. The teacher also enjoys the liberty of showing particular segments at conference time if the parents need more description as to their children's behavior or progress.

Many teachers also use checklists and inventories to assess student progress.

Many teachers also use checklists and inventories to assess student progress. These tools provide a simple and clear way to demonstrate growth over time. Using the same checklist or inventory throughout the program (i.e., twice each year) provides a consistent description of the child's development. An excellent example of a reading comprehension checklist can be found on page 72.

Individual Anecdotal Record Form

Run off a stack of these forms and keep them—one for each student in your class—in a three-ring binder. Make your notes on the appropriate form. When a page is filled up, it can be replaced with a new page and the filled page placed in the student's portfolio. No time is lost in transcribing information!

Individual Anecdotal Record

Name _____

Date	Comment

Reprinted from TCM 504 Portfolios and Other Assessments, *Teacher Created Materials, 1993*

Individual Checklist for Literal Comprehension in Reading

Use this checklist to document your observation of literal comprehension in first or second grade readers.

Grade 1 or 2

Name _____ Date _____

Title of Story _____

Behavior	Observed Poor to Excellent			
	1	2	3	4
Can answer questions about details from the story (literal details).				
Can retell story, including all main events (main idea).				
Can retell story in chronological order (sequence).				
Can answer questions about first, last, etc. (sequence).				
Defines words from the story (vocabulary).				
Recognizes and explains effects of affix on a word in the story (vocabulary).				

Reprinted from TCM 504 Portfolios and Other Assessments, *Teacher Created Materials, 1993*

Portfolios

Portfolios are a common method teachers are using to document student progress. While teachers used to fill grade books with percentages and letter grades, they are now attempting to assess students more authentically by building a portfolio to represent the accomplishments of each child.

Portfolios complement the learning center classroom philosophy in many ways. First, they respect individual differences by viewing the child as an individual, assessing his or her needs, regardless of the work of others. Second, they involve the child in the evaluation and planning processes (Graves & Sunstein, 1992). Third, they encourage risk taking, respect cooperative work, and enhance self-esteem. Finally, they develop a sense of responsibility as students take pride in ownership and accomplishment.

Student Involvement

A key element in assessment, especially when using portfolios, is involving students in the process. This is fairly simple when used with learning centers, as teachers can assist students in becoming evaluators of their own progress. Many teachers choose to build an assessment component into each learning center, while some opt to ask students to reflect and evaluate at a particular center on a frequent basis. Either way, these self-evaluations provide a clear picture of how the child views his or her progress, and they assist each student in building reflection skills and self-confidence.

Parent Involvement

Another key element in assessment is involving parents in the process by reporting/communicating with them on a regular basis. Parents are partners in education and need to play a significant role in the determination of goals and expectations for their children. Learning centers can easily be created, modified, or changed to meet the individual needs of each child. By assessing parents' beliefs and communicating frequently, teachers can include parents in the most precious experience of their children's lives—their education.

Parent reflections are wonderful assessment tools and are extremely valuable in meeting the needs of each child. Many teachers assess parents at the beginning of each year to find out what parents' goals are for their children. Teachers also assess informally on a daily basis via parent meetings and phone calls. Whether it be standing in the parking lot as students leave each day or setting specific times for appointments, successful teaching requires successful communication. Parents need to be involved in order to best assist in the education of their children.

> **Portfolios are a common method teachers are using to document student progress.**

Concluding Remarks

Two principles that form the basis of successful assessment in a classroom are authenticity and structure. Real assessment can readily occur in an environment that is organized for learning. Although a learning center classroom may at first glance appear unstructured, it is in fact highly organized and prepared to meet the needs of each student. When the program runs smoothly, with details worked out and expectations clear, the opportunities for authentic assessment are numerous.

Authentic assessment is the preferred approach and works particularly well in a learning center environment. Strategies involve all participants; the teacher, student, and parent work collectively to meet specific learning needs. Examples of authentic assessment tools include writing samples, tape-recorded reading samples, videotaped samples, teacher observations, anecdotal records, checklists and inventories, student reflections, and parent evaluations. The use of portfolios is an excellent method for collecting student work. Portfolios provide an invaluable record and display of student accomplishments.

> **It is important for the student and parent to play a role in the assessment process.**

It is important for the student and parent to play a role in the assessment process. Both must share in the experience and be valued as participants. This thoughtful, sensitive, and supportive relationship among teachers, parents, and students is a prerequisite for learning and will ensure a high rate of success for students.

References

Carle, E. (1977). <u>The grouchy ladybug</u>. New York: HarperCollins Publishers.

Cole, J. (1990). <u>The magic school bus inside the solar system</u>. New York: Scholastic.

Gardner, H. (1985). <u>Frames of mind: The theory of multiple intelligences</u>. New York: Basic Books.

Glasser, W. (1990). <u>Quality school: Managing students without coercion</u>. New York: Harper & Row.

Goodlad, J. I., & Oakes, J. (1988, February). We must offer equal access to knowledge. <u>Educational Leadership 8</u>, 16–22.

Goodman, Y. M. (1978). Kid watching: An alternative to testing. <u>National Elementary Principal, 57</u>(4), 41–45.

Graves, D. H., & Sunstein, B. S. (Eds.). (1992). <u>Portfolio portraits</u>. Portsmouth, NH: Heinemann.

Hallahan, D. P., & Kauffman, J. M. (1994). <u>Exceptional children</u>. Needham Heights, MA: Allyn & Bacon.

Huyett, B. (1994, Summer). Early childhood education: Involving the special needs child in learning centers. <u>Day Care & Early Education 21</u>(4), 43–44.

Jasmine, G. (1995). <u>Early Childhood Assessment</u>. Westminster, CA: Teacher Created Materials.

Jasmine, J. (1993). <u>Portfolios and other assessments</u>. Westminster, CA: Teacher Created Materials.

Johnston, H., James, S., Barnes, B., & Colton, T. (1978). <u>The learning center ideabook: Activities for the elementary and middle grades</u>. Boston: Allyn & Bacon, Inc.

Kantrowitz, B., & Wingert, P. (1989, April, 17). How kids learn. <u>Newsweek</u>, 50–57.

Kaska, K. (1987). <u>The wolf's chicken stew</u>. New York: G. P. Putnam's Sons.

Lazear, D. (1991). <u>Seven ways of teaching</u>. Palatine, IL: Skylight.

Martin, B., Jr. (1983). <u>Brown bear, brown bear, what do you see</u>? New York: Henry Holt.

McClay, J. L. (1996). <u>The multi-age classroom</u>. Westminster, CA: Teacher Created Materials.

Neill, D. M., & Medina, N. J. (1989, May). Standardized testing: Harmful to educational health. <u>Phi Delta Kappan, 70</u>(9), 688–697.

Opitz, M. (1995, January). Self-assessment and learning centers: Do they go together? <u>Teaching PreK–8, 25</u>(4), 104–106.

Opitz, M. F. (1994). <u>Learning centers: Getting them started, keeping them going</u>. New York: Scholastic, Inc.

Pattillo, J., & Vaughan, E. (1992). <u>Learning centers for child-centered classrooms</u>. Washington, DC: National Education Association of the United States.

Petreshene, S. S. (1978). <u>The complete guide to learning centers</u>. Palo Alto, CA: Pendragon House, Inc.

Pfau, N., & Zeddun, S. (1995). <u>Teaching basic skills through literature: Math</u>. Westminster, CA: Teacher Created Materials.

Poppe, C. A., & Van Matre, N. A. (1985). <u>Science learning centers for the primary grades</u>. West Nyack, NY: The Center for Applied Research in Education, Inc.

Province of British Columbia Ministry of Education. (1991). <u>Supporting learning...understanding and assessing progress of children in the primary program</u>. British Columbia, Canada: Author.

Routman, R. (1991). <u>Invitations: Changing as teachers and learners K–12</u>. Portsmouth, NH: Heinemann.

Ryan, C. D. (1994). <u>Authentic assessment</u>. Westminster, CA: Teacher Created Materials.

Thomas, J. I. (1975). <u>Learning centers: Opening up the classroom</u>. Boston: Holbrook Press.

United States Department of Labor, The Secretary's Commission on Achieving Necessary Skills. (1994). <u>What work requires of schools: A SCANS report for America 2000</u>. Washington, DC: U.S. Government Printing Office.

Wait, S. S., & Stephens, K. (1989, May). Center your reading instruction. <u>Instructor, 98</u>(9), 42–45.

Wallace, A. H. (1993). <u>Learning centers through the year</u>. Westminster, CA: Teacher Created Materials.

Teacher Created Materials Resource List

TCM 059 Learning Centers Through the Year

TCM 147 Activities for Any Literature Unit

TCM 206 Whole Language Units for Predictable Books

TCM 342 Connecting Math & Literature

TCM 504 Portfolios and Other Assessments

TCM 651 Cooperative Learning Activities for Language Arts

TCM 773 Language Arts Assessment: Grades 1–2

TCM 790 Teaching Basic Skills Through Literature: Math

TCM 1000 Weather Learning Center

TCM 1042 Sea Life Learning Center

TCM 1043 Creepy Crawlies Learning Center